THE NEW CHINA:
A CATHOLIC RESPONSE

Edited by
Michael Chu, S.J.

The Catholic
Theological Union
LIBRARY
Chicago, Ill.

D0770086

PAULIST PRESS
New York / Ramsey / Toronto

ABBREVIATIONS

Båstad: Theological Implications of the New China. Papers presented at the ecumenical seminar held in Båstad, Sweden, January 29 to February 2, 1974 (Lutheran World Federation/Pro Mundi Vita: Geneva and Brussels, 1974).

Louvain: Christian Faith and the Chinese Explerience. Papers and Reports from an Ecumenical Colloquium held in Louvain, Belgium, September 9 to 14, 1974 (Lutheran World Federation/Pro Mundi Vita: Geneva and Brussels, 1974).

Copyright © 1977 by
Michael Chu, S.J.

All rights reserved. No part of this book may be reproduced or transmitted in any form or by any means, electronic or mechanical, including photocopying, recording or by any information storage and retrieval system without permission in writing from the Publisher.

Library of Congress
Catalog Card Number: 76-56958

ISBN: 0-8091-2004-6

Cover Design: Morris Berman

Published by Paulist Press
Editorial Office: 1865 Broadway, N.Y., N.Y. 10023
Business Office: 545 Island Road, Ramsey, N.J. 07446

Printed and bound in the
United States of America

Contents

Introduction

In 1949 Mao Tse-tung won his victory and set about forming the New China. Sent by Christ to bring the good news to all the world, the Church must be interested in this New China. Seemingly, however, the good news cannot be proclaimed to one fourth of the human race. More than that, Mao's China aims to create its own form of "new man," to find salvation simply within this world, and to become a model for all developing countries. In the social, economic and political fields the New China has won stunning successes. All of these facts present a series of questions which Christian thinkers cannot ignore.

In 1974 two groups of scholars and theologians—both Protestant and Catholic—met in Bästad (Sweden) and Louvain (Belgium) to discuss the theological implications of the New China. They saw Mao and Maoism as representing an authentic and daring challenge to Christianity.

In 1975 several theologians at the Gregorian University in Rome continued the discussions inaugurated at Båstad and Louvain. This book contains the results. Robert Faricy deals with "Mao's thought and Christian belief," offering his own interpretation of faith and ideology in the light of the New China. Domenico Grasso reflects on "the new China and God's plan for salvation," paying particular attention to three issues: the nature of salvation, the concept of the "new man" and the divine plan of salvation. Francis Sullivan tackles the theological implications of the New China for an understanding of the Christian Church as the "Universal Sacrament of Salvation." Gerald O'Collins takes up the theme of "Christ and China," examining first the significance of suffering and the emulation of heroes in China. Then he asks the question: What emerges from a confrontation between the two figures, Mao and Jesus?

Two further contributions greatly enrich this book. From

1

Yale University, Julia Ching provides a comprehensive setting for the subsequent papers. She situates the book within current Christian attempts both to ponder Christian failures in China and to rethink the Christian message in terms of what we now know of the New China. Paul Rule, who teaches Chinese studies at La Trobe University in Australia and visited China in mid-1975, considers the questions: Does Maoism offer an opening to genuine transcendence? Is it a truly religious movement?

The New China:
A Dialectical Response

JULIA CHING

In the past few years we have witnessed a growing interest in the subject of China and Christianity. There have been many study sessions, discussions and colloquia. Of these, the best known are the two conferences organized by Pro Mundi Vita, a Catholic research and information center based in Belgium, and the Department of Studies of the Lutheran World Federation (Geneva, Switzerland). I refer here to the conferences which took place at Båstad, Sweden (January, 1974) and at Louvain, Belgium (September, 1974). These joint ecumenical endeavors in understanding China's meaning for Christian theology have aroused many responses. Our book, *The New China: A Catholic Response,* comes as one such group reflection. This is essentially the thoughtful response of a group of Jesuit theologians, professors at the Pontifical Gregorian University in Rome. Although they have no direct experience of China, they have decided to take up the challenge of the New China to probe deeper into their own faith. They do so without the emotional involvement of missionaries who had been in China or who would like to be in China, and yet with a sympathy for those who have had this experience or who still look forward to an alternative form of serving the Chinese people. They bring to their task the trained expertise of professional theologians and the concern of believers. The result is another step forward in the continuing dialogue: a dialogue among these men themselves, as well as with the participants at the Båstad and Louvain conferences, a dialogue with the reading public, and—besides—an invitation to all concerned to engage in a common dialogue with the Lord of history.

3

The theologians at the Gregorian University invited two lay persons to share in their effort of theological reflection and dialogue. They are Paul Rule, an Australian scholar who recently visited China and has done important research on the early Jesuit missions there, and Julia Ching, born in China, a convert to Christianity and a participant at the Båstad and Louvain conferences, whose specialization is Chinese philosophy and religion. Hence this book can claim to be "catholic" in two ways: according to the ecclesiastical definition of the word, as well as through the varied national origins and geographical distribution of the contributors.

Speaking generally, this book resembles the earlier *Theological Implications of the New China* (Geneva & Brussels, 1974), to which it serves as a response by the particular methodology it has adopted. Care is taken to situate the collective effort of reflection against a broader background of other attempts, especially by clearly defining the problem and by delineating the areas of common ground. A comparative analysis then follows, expounding Mao Tse-tung's thought within the general Marxist framework and examining it in the light of Christian beliefs. This philosophical effort (Faricy) precedes the more specifically theological response which seeks especially to relate the new China to the divine plan for salvation (Grasso, Sullivan), to the meaning of suffering and emulation of suffering heroes, especially of Jesus Christ (O'Collins), as well as to the Church's self-understanding (Sullivan).

The reader will find certain common features in the contributions included here. There is a sincerity and openness to the problem of China, as it is perceived by Catholic theologians. There is a concerted effort to find positive significance in the experience of the Chinese Revolution, albeit with a note of caution, on account of the acknowledged inadequacy of available knowledge of China. And there is hope expressed for more dialogue among Christians concerning China, and for a future in which dialogue with China herself may become possible and useful to both Christianity and China. Such hope is always grounded in the belief in divine guidance of history as well as in a concern for China's own well-being.

Nevertheless, the book claims only to be *a* Catholic response to the new China. The theologians are conscious of their responsibility as interpreters of a major Christian faith. But they have collaborated to produce this book in the hope of interesting other Catholics, indeed, other Christians, to continue the dialogue in a meaningful way. They have also done so with careful cognizance of expressed Chinese views, especially Chinese Christian views. The invitation is also extended to them to participate in an endeavor which may perhaps contribute also to the fulfillment of hopes for deeper theological reflection and expression within a Chinese frame of reference—here including a Chinese cultural matrix and a Chinese experience of the Communist Revolution, whether positive or negative, as well as a genuinely Chinese pride in the China of yesterday, today and tomorrow.

The Problem: China and Christianity

As the person responsible for situating this study against a more general background, I see my task especially in terms of the clarification of the problem itself: the problem of the new China, and the problem of "common ground" between this China and the Christian religion. I shall seek to define China's meaning for Christianity as well as Christianity's meaning for China before going on to define the intellectual situation confronting us today: the meaning of Maoism, the reasons for its attractiveness, as well as the need of remembering that the "New China" need not be *exclusively* identified with its present leader and his interpretation of Marxist ideology. I shall then pose certain problems myself, both to the contributors of this book as well as to its readers, problems concerning the theological response to the new China, which are also the central concern of this book.

There are, however, certain difficulties that should be pointed out in the beginning. The first obvious difficulty is that of defining the problem. Both China and Christianity are vast subjects. China may be considered variously—or all at once—as a geopolitical reality, an ethnic-cultural tradition, a large segment of the world's population or a socialist ideology contending with remarkable success for a position of leadership with Moscow, the center of alleged Marxist orthodoxy. On the other hand, Christianity may evoke the image of "Christendom" or post-Christendom extending over diverse nations, mostly of the Caucasion race and European origin, and in the case of the Catholic Church with its seat of power in Rome. Christianity may also bring to mind a Latin past, much of which is still with us. Christianity may mean post-Vatican II theology, but it may also mean post-Vatican II diplomacy.

For all practical purposes, the new China refers in our context either to the country itself today or to the dominant ideology there known to the West as Maoism, while Christianity refers sometimes to Christian faith in general, and sometimes to the Catholic Church in particular. Such flexibility is necessitated by the vast nature of the issues under discussion. Therefore, instead of dwelling upon the difficulties of precise definitions, I shall continue by offering some answers to the meaning of China for Christianity and of Christianity for China.

What does China mean to Christianity, and what does Christianity mean to China? These seem to me questions which need to be answered when we discuss the meaning of Christian faith in the light of the Chinese experience.

The first question, what China means to Christianity, may be better answered when we first understand what China means to the Chinese themselves. And since we are considering in particular the experience of the Chinese Communist Revolution, I shall quote from Chairman Mao himself:

China is one of the largest countries in the world, her territory being about the size of the whole of Europe. In this vast country of ours . . . our forefathers have labored, lived and multiplied. . . . Throughout the history of Chinese civilization its agriculture and handicrafts have been renowned for their high levels of development; there have been many great thinkers, scientists, inventors, statesmen, soldiers, men of letters and artists, and we have a rich store of classical works. . . . Thus China has one of the oldest civilizations in the world; she has a recorded history of nearly 4,000 years.[1]

Every country considers itself, and rightly so, as unique. China is no exception. But for the extent of her land, her large population—one fourth of the world's—and her position as an historical center for the East Asian civilization, China feels that she cannot be compared, as a country and a people, with any other on the same level. China considered herself, for thousands of years, a civilization rather than a nation. It would be more reasonable therefore to compare China with the whole of Western Europe than with any Western country. I say this not out of chauvinism, but to communicate a sense of the Chinese self-image. This should help us to understand why China has never shown much interest in European culture or religion and also why China, in the present, seems exclusively concerned with her own ideology and problems, even after having accepted Marx-Leninism from the West.

What does China mean to Christianity? I can say quite openly that in the past it has always represented to the Christian imagination, a land of paganism, a people to be converted. In opposition to "Chinese universalism," the feeling of the Chinese that their country is the center of the world, that they have much to give and teach and little to receive and learn from the rest of the world, we find this strong sense of "Christian universalism" for which the Christian faith alone can serve as axis of a religious universe. The problem was that the Chinese took little trouble to spread their culture, content to teach only those who came to her doors, while the Christians were much more active and dynamic in propagating their religion. And since Christians were—and have been—mostly Europeans, the Christian sense of "universalism" was easily to become part and parcel of a geopolitical outlook.

I consider it important to compare the Jesuit missions of the 16th/18th centuries in China with the later Catholic and Protestant missions of the 19th/20th centuries which were associated with Western imperialism.[2] There are obvious differences. As is known to all those familiar with mission history, the Jesuits of Matteo Ricci's time came to China as guests, ready to exchange ideas with the Chinese. But the modern missionaries, both Catholic and Protestant, appeared as representatives of a "superior religious faith" supported by political and military power. Yet the Jesuit mission in China was doomed to failure because of the Rites controversy and the later suppression of the Society. The modern missions of the 19th and 20th centuries would also, in their own turn, meet with failure partly through a lack of basic understanding between the missionaries and the people they were trying to convert, and perhaps also through the Chinese hatred for foreigners which linked the missionaries to the imperialists. And now, it appears that all previous missionary attempts to win China over to Christianity have backfired: China remains not only unconverted but even antagonistic to the Christian faith. And what is more, in our recent years, the example of the Chinese Revolution has appeared to gain so much in popularity as to challenge once more Christian self-confidence and self-sufficiency. China seems to have done well enough for herself and to have become a symbol of hope for oppressed peoples all over the world at the time when institutional churches are wondering about their own uncertain futures in a secularized world.

And yet, China remains important for the Western Christian who even feels a sense of guilt-complex with regard to mission history, and wishes to consider seriously the ideological challenge presented by Maoism. This continues to be true, in spite of the apparent indifference with which the Chinese Communists respond to religious questions. For them, Christianity was definitely linked with cultural and political imperialism, and Chinese Christians are considered somehow unpatriotic for having accepted the religion of the imperialists. But the number of Chinese Christians is too small for the present government to worry too much about, especially as the official measures to limit and suppress religious activities appear to have been successful. For the Communists, Christianity does not present an important problem. Feuerbach, Marx and Engels have already solved the problem philosophically.[3] Since the exodus of the missionaries, Christianity has become once more almost invisible in China.

THE INTELLECTUAL SITUATION TODAY

1. What Is Maoism?

What is Maoism? Is it essentially similar to Marxist-Leninist theory or is it not? What has Mao taken over from Marx and Lenin, and adapted and transformed?

In order to understand Maoism, we must remember that Mao began his career as a traditionally oriented nationalist, who desired to tear down the old hierarchical social structure as well as break down the hold of a fossilized religious and value system over a long suffering people. He wanted to free their energy for the construction of a new China. After two decades of learning, he developed the ability to use Leninist revolutionary techniques toward the attainment of this end by uniting these with the struggle of the Chinese countryside. He mobilized the peasant masses in the name of class solidarity against the landowners, and in the name of national solidarity against the Japanese aggressors. Then came the leap from guerrilla warfare to the building of a modern industrial society.[4]

In the People's Republic, the word Maoism does not appear. In its place is the expression, "the Thought of Mao Tsetung." It signifies a special way of thinking as this is presented and reflected upon in the writings, speeches and instructions of Chairman Mao. The starting-point is a statement made by Mao in 1938: that there is no such thing as an abstract Marxism, that there is only a concrete Marxism which has assumed a national form, namely, by being adapted to a concrete struggle in the concrete conditions of China. The ideal of guerrilla warfare becomes typical for such a Chinese form of Marx-Leninism—especially the union of theory and practice, and self-reliance on political, military and economic levels. The ideal Communist is worker, farmer, soldier and student, all in one, with full equality of man and woman.

As I have already mentioned, the Chinese Communists have been content, in their critical analysis of religion, to take over from Feuerbach, Marx and Engels, the Projection and Fantasy theories. They have not themselves made any particular contribution in this regard. But since the religious situation in China is different from that of Western Europe or Russia, they have also associated Christianity and its missions with Western imperialism. The native religions, such as Buddhism and Taoism, became associated with the oppressive mentality of the "feudal ages," while Confucianism, a philosophy with religious overtones, also came under strong attack.

Let me quote here what Mao and his comrades said in 1939 about religious cultural aggression:

The imperialist powers have never slackened their efforts to poison the minds of the Chinese people. This is their policy of cultural aggression. And it is carried out through missionary work, through establishing hospitals and schools, publishing newspapers and inducing Chinese students to study abroad. Their aim is to train intellectuals who will serve their interests and to dupe the people.[5]

Christianity is therefore unwelcome on two grounds: as religion and as a form of cultural imperialism. Moreover, religion is itself quite useless. Its place has been taken over by a political consciousness, as given in the Communist ideology. "Not to have a correct political point of view is like having no soul."[6]

2. Why Is Maoism So Attractive?

In spite of the claims pressed forward by Maoists, the Chairman has manifested little talent as an abstract thinker. He is essentially a man of action and a revolutionary leader. But then, why has Maoism become so attractive?

The answer lies in its romantic appeal. If one may borrow images from myth and history at the same time, it may be said that this appeal lies in Mao's combination of Prometheus and Garibaldi. The Promethean urge represents the Marxist in him, the Garibaldi side represents the patriot and nationalist, with a flair for drama. True, the Promethean image is a very Western one, quite alien to the Chinese mind. But Mao has been able to project this image on the Chinese imagination by uniting it with the nationalist desire for self-determination, for becoming a modern, industrialized state. Besides, he has done so less through pedantic discourses than through his appeal to classical examples or folk stories in the Chinese tradition. A well-known parable is that of the Foolish Old Man who could remove mountains. It is taken from a Taoist work, *Lieh-tzu:*

An old man . . . lived in northern China long, long ago and was known as the Foolish Old Man of North Mountain. His house faced south and beyond his doorway stood the two great peaks . . . obstructing the way. He called his sons; and, hoe in hand, they began to dig up these mountains with great determination. Another greybeard, known as the Wise Old Man, saw them and said derisively, "How silly of you to do this! It is quite impossible for you few to dig up these two huge mountains." The Foolish Old Man replied, "When I die, my sons will carry on; when they die, there will be my grandsons, and then their sons and grandsons, and so on. . . . High as they are, the mountains cannot grow any higher and with every bit we dig, they will be that much lower. Why can't we clear them away?" Having refuted the Wise Old Man's wrong view, he went on digging every day, unshaken in his conviction. God was moved by this, and he sent down two angels, who carried the mountains away on their backs.[7]

Originally, the moral of this parable lay in a sense of perseverance, a characteristic Chinese virtue. The appeal of removing mountains and of God's help to the persevering is one addressed to the human imagination—as is frequently found in Taoist writings. There was at first no question of a Promethean urge to dominate nature, just as no such urge may be said to exist in the Gospels, when Christ spoke of faith in God:

> For truly, I say to you, if you have faith as a grain of mus-
> tard seed, you will say to this mountain "Move from here
> to there," and it will move; and nothing will be impossible
> to you. (Mt 17:20)

> Have faith in God! Truly, I say to you, whoever says to
> this mountain, "Be taken up and cast into the sea," and
> does not doubt in his heart, but believes that what he says
> will come to pass, it will be done for him. (Mk 11:22-23)

Mao, however, has given the parable a Promethean emphasis, by stressing the moving of the mountains. For him, the two
peaks represent imperialism and feudalism. As we know, the
word "feudalism" has a technical meaning in the Communist
usage—referring to social-economic structures as well as religious attitudes which prevent humankind's domination of nature. But where Marxists are usually content with the diviriza-
tion of people as such, Mao has gone one step further—by
identifying the Chinese masses as God:

> The Chinese Communist Party has long made up its mind
> to dig up (the two mountains). We must persevere and
> work unceasingly, and we too, will touch God's heart. Our
> God is none other than the masses of the Chinese people. If
> they stand up and dig together with us, why can't these two
> mountains be cleared away?[8]

Besides, in referring to the mountains as representing imperialism and feudalism, Mao has also demonstrated a definite
nationalist feeling, together with an anti-Western impetus. For
where Lenin was a European interested above all in world revolution, Mao is an Asian, for whom nationalism is no necessary
evil, but rather a value in itself. On account of Mao's achievements, China has already become the precursor as well as ex-
emplar for revolution in Asia, Africa and Latin America. In a

strange way, China remains the "Middle Country"—the center of attention for the Third World.[9]

3. Maoist Voluntarism

Together with the Promethean urge and the divinization of the Chinese People—rather than of humanity as such—we find in the Parable of the Foolish Old Man as interpreted by Mao Tse-tung a strong undertone of voluntarism. This voluntarism is characteristic of the Chinese who have been able to survive many odds in their long history. It is also typical of Marx-Leninism, especially as emphasized by Mao himself. In the parable just mentioned, for example, the truly wise man is not the man of reason, but a man of will and decision, whom the world regarded as foolish. Certainly, Mao considers himself the personification of the "foolish, yet wise man." Such a man needs no faith in God or the gods. But he is able, with perseverance and the support of his whole clan, to move mountains.

In this light, the myth of the Long March also becomes very meaningful. It is an historical fact that the Chinese Communist soldiers, under the leadership of Mao and others, undertook a Long March of about 6,000 miles from the mountains of Kiangsi in the east to their new guerrilla headquarters in Yenan, northern Shensi. This Long March began in October 1934 and ended one year later. It was made necessary by Chiang Kai-shek's anti-Communist campaigns. Certainly, it gives testimony to human hardiness and endurance. All along the way, the Red Army was harassed not only by Chiang's forces, but also by nomadic tribes of minority ethnic groups in the interior of China, and by the very terrain and geography itself, especially a long stretch of marshes where sleep on the ground was impossible, and where a large number died. Only 30,000 of the 300,000 people survived this March.[10]

It is no surprise that this historical event should have become a myth[11] for the Chinese Communist Party in its task of directing the country and the people to the goal of becoming a modern and industrialized nation. And once more, as in the parable of the Foolish Old Man, what is exalted is human endurance, the spirit of sacrifice. The fact that Mao should have taken over the Party leadership during the time of the Long March also made it symbolic of his continued leadership of the Party and the people.

But then, one may ask, why such a voluntarism? Why so much enthusiasm for a seemingly prosaic goal—the construction of a modern industrialized state? This may represent, all the more, a problem to those of us who have become tired of over-industrialization in the West, where the utopia remains ever further from realization and where, instead, ecological problems have been pressing for solutions.

Why so much voluntarism? One reason for this feature of the Chinese ideology is to be found in China's situation as an underdeveloped country, which manifests an atmosphere of impatience—a burning wish to change everything overnight. This is strengthened in Mao by his flair for struggle and drama.[12]

CONCLUSIONS

The Ambiguity of Maoism and of the Chinese Experience

In my opinion, the Chinese experience of the Communist Revolution remains ambiguous. On the one hand, the successful socialist revolution in China has inspired liberation movements everywhere. China has become a symbol of hope for oppressed peoples everywhere in the world, encouraging and promoting—quite unconsciously on her part—Christian theologies of revolution and liberation in Europe as well as in Latin America. China can no longer remain unnoticed, not even by those churches or theological circles, which have little missionary involvement. On the other hand, our knowledge and information about China are very inadequate. We do not have even precise figures for the Chinese population. We continue to wonder why

Confucius and Lin Piao have been criticized together in the recent past, and our ignorance regarding Christianity in China is all the more shocking. We hear of a near-complete absence of institutionalized religious activity, and of an open support of churchmen in China for the government's religious policies. There are no known protest groups among Christians in China, as there are in South Korea or the Philippines. If China inspires protest and revolution outside of her borders, she appears unwilling to tolerate any open criticism of the Leader himself and his way of governing.[13]

What is the new China—a myth, or a reality? As long as our knowledge remains so scanty, the task of interpretation is extremely difficult. Yet we cannot merely wait until such information as we need may come to us. Rather, it seems important to acknowledge this ambiguity and not to seize upon what appears to be good or bad in China today. For example, where the government has succeeded in giving the people a sense of "collective freedom" from imperialism and from famine, it does not appear to have given much attention to the promotion of individual freedom. Even if the Chinese are free to criticize other Party members, who are not sufficiently "Maoist," they have not been permitted to criticize the Leader himself.

Mao is now eighty-two years old. He is a complex personality, a man who is full of contradictions which he does not conceal. According to Stuart Schram he represents a mixture of Lenin—with an instinctive sense for organization as political weapon—and Garibaldi—the romantic Italian revolutionary and nationalist. His quest is basically one of adventure as well as of socialist revolution. He wishes to set free the energy of the masses, seeing himself as the incorporation of their will. Even if we are concerned with Maoism as such, we must remember that there is a China—a socialist China—without Mao and after Mao. Mao has struggled his whole life, coping at every stage with new ideas and new situations. Having begun his career as a revolutionary iconoclast against the traditional social inhibitions and obstructions, he finds himself today confronting the problem of constructing an industrial society in the age of automation. Like Alexander the Great, Mao has discovered that

the world which he wishes to conquer, is no longer there—
because it is no longer the same as the one he used to know.[14]
What kind of socialist China will survive Mao, perhaps even
prosper after him? This is the question that many people are
asking.

A More Open Theology?

A reflection over the Chinese experience of the socialist
revolution may lead us to reflect on the question of a more open
theology, a theology that is not so self-preoccupied. By "self-
preoccupation," I refer to the tendency to see everything
through "theological spectacles" prejudging certain issues a
priori according to definite theological categories, which have
meaning only for those who use them, as well as the impossi-
bility of thinking in other conceptual frameworks.

It seems to me that in the past, such self-preoccupation had
led to the wrong judgments made during the Rites controversy,
and to the cultural imperialism of the 19th and 20th century
missions. It was all the result of triumphalism. Such an attitude
showed itself in principles like "Outside the Church no Salvation" as well as in more recent attempts to regard non-Christians as anonymous Christians in order to "save" them according to theological language. These are all one-sided judgments.
A non-Christian could turn the sentence around and say, for example: "Outside the Church no Salvation, because no Sin and
so no need for Salvation."

With reference to the Chinese Revolution, this theological
self-preoccupation expresses itself in two ways: by trying to
"christianize" Maoism and by an exaggerated compunction or
guilt-complex. The Roman Congregation for the Propagation of
the Faith has published a statement through the Fides News
Service (April 4, 1973), declaring that Mao's thought contains
Christian reflections. It affirms—and correctly so—that,
through accepting Marxism, China has also opened itself, for
the first time in its existence, to certain Christian ideas, and that
China speaks of such important human values as a spirit of pov-

erty, of sacrifice and renunciation. It also makes reference to some of Mao's directives as the "most authentic expression of the social doctrine of the Church" and even of the Second Vatican Council. It concludes with the hope that the social encyclicals as well as the Council documents have not remained unknown even to the government at Peking. I shall quote only one paragraph:

> Communism excels in making its own all that may serve its objectives. This is why one finds in Mao directives which may well be integrated in the great moral principles of the thousand year old civilization of China and also serve as the most authentic expression of the social doctrine of the Church.[15]

I should like, however, to turn the question around and ask: Cannot "the other side" also say that the Christian religion is always seeking to make its own, and appropriate, all that it finds to be congenial in other societies and traditions? Is not the entire idea of missionary adaptation based on this premise?

I am not excluding the possibility or value of missionary adaptation. I think, however, that some of its premises may require re-examination. But I wish to mention here some of the ways in which a "Christianization" of Mao thought has been attempted, for example at the Båstad and Louvain conferences, in order to point out the obvious risks of superficial comparisons which are based on little factual knowledge. It seems to me unnecessary to "christianize" Mao in order to understand or appreciate him. It seems to me that dialogue does not require the other partner to accept one's own vocabulary or categories, but rather that both partners should use a *common* language—for example, one based on common *human* values rather than what must be called *Christian* values.

By Christianization of Maoism, I refer to the identification of China with the Kingdom of God on earth, and attempts to regard Mao as China's savior, a kind of new Moses. An example is this statement of Joseph Needham:

> The Chinese society of the present day . . . is further on
> the way to the true society of mankind, the Kingdom of
> God, if you like, than our own. I think China is the only
> true Christian country in the world in the present day, in
> spite of its absolute rejection of all religion. . . . Where is
> Christ to be found? . . . Where the good are, and where
> good things are done. . . . That means appreciating what
> is happening in China at the present day.[16]

The metaphor of the Kingdom of God takes the goal of
spiritual fulfillment for a believing people, as well as the idea of
a political utopia, simply in Christian terms. Nevertheless, even
Thomas More's ideal society, the *classical* Utopia, was described as a non-Christian society without the trappings of
Christian euphemisms. To call the good "Christian" is actually
a kind of cultural condescension, even though it is being done
by the best-minded persons.

I acknowledge that there may be something in common between the Long March and the Jewish exodus—even if the latter
appeared to have lasted a longer time. But what about Mao as a
new Moses? Is it not too early to praise Mao so unequivocally,
before a judgment of history can be reached? Is this also not the
language which does not really make sense to the Chinese themselves, who are neither Jews nor Christians? Is not also a certain
"idolization" of Mao possible, while he is still in power, and the
outside world is yet without sufficient information about all that
has passed, and is passing in China itself? Mao has openly
spoken *against* an exaggerated personality cult that exalts him
above other human beings. Perhaps Christians may take this to
heart too.

Instead of seeking to christianize Maoism, is it not perhaps
better to understand and appreciate what is *basic* to Maoism
and to the Chinese image of people and of the world, which
Maoism itself has inherited? I refer to the Chinese sense of optimism in human nature—an optimism which persists today
despite the official rejection of Mencius' philosophy of original
human goodness, and its preference for Hsun-tzu's teaching of
original human wickedness. Even for Hsun-tzu, human beings

are capable of reform and perfection—through education. Maoist education itself is based on its acceptance of human perfectibility.

In this regard, it is important to point out that the contributors to this volume have indicated clearly the importance of understanding salvation in scriptural terms, and of denying the validity of any easy identification of the new China with the Kingdom of God (Grasso). There is need, indeed, of finding an uneasy balance between de-Westernization of certain theological categories and firm adherence to the scriptural foundations of Christian belief and Christian theology.

Then, also, free from the emotional involvement of former missionaries, the contributors to this book have been able to analyze objectively the significance of the missionary's endeavor and his share of suffering and of persecution (O'Collins). Effort has also been made to define the Church in broad terms, identifying her with the work of God's Spirit rather than appropriating the Spirit exclusively to her (Sullivan). Such effort of self-understanding is also an application of learning from the Chinese experience that sees church authority also as standing in a complementary unity of opposites with the Christian faithful—a unity strengthened by communication between the leadership and the masses and based always on love (Faricy).

It is this communication that we all seek to encourage—not only vertical communication, but also horizontal. Theology, after all, is essentially communication: the interpretation of God's Word and the dissemination of this message. But this interpretation and this dissemination can only be valid when realized in the full context of human history.

Today, China studies stand to gain somewhat from the readiness of Christians elsewhere to accept certain elements in the Marxist view of humanity, society and history that are not entirely antagonistic to Christian belief. The question now is no longer one of polarization. Humbled and open, Christians are more ready to learn all they can from the great socialist experiment in China, discerning in it a religious sense of commitment and purpose that responds to their own inner stirrings.

For this progress in self-criticism and in learning from the

Marxists a sense of social and political responsibility, Christians
are to be congratulated. But excess in one direction or the other
should be avoided. Excessive remorse about the past cannot
lead to conversions, whether of oneself or of others, and may
even obscure reality. Excess cannot contribute to an accurate
assessment of past missionary successes and failures, unless self-
criticism itself yields to rational analysis. Has the failure of missions been simply the result of the missionary's political involvement with the imperialist powers? This historical factor ought
not be denied. But were there not other, equally important, fac-
tors? Was there not also a sense of racial, cultural and religious
superiority—the result of ignorance of China and her own traditions and self-image? Following some adulation of China by
18th century Europe, there was a European and American arro-
gance in the 19th and 20th centuries regarding China's pre-
scientific worldview and pre-industrialized society, as well as
China's alleged cultural and historical stagnation. How many
Chinese became Christian converts in order to separate themselves from their Chinese past and to earn self-esteem by the
adoption of a Western life-style, and in order to make friends
among the privileged in China—the Westerners and their
friends in high society? If, in the long run, these changes contributed in part to China's growth in self-reliance, it should be
pointed out that this was only restored in isolation from the
West, and in defiance of both the West and China's own cultural heritage.

The Christian is also to be praised for his readiness to collaborate with the Marxist, to enter into a living dialogue with
him. But whether the political and social ideology, which claims
credit for the vast improvements in living conditions in today's
China, as compared with the old order that prevailed in the
past, has also been responsible for subjecting the people's welfare to itself, for hindering further improvements, is also subject
to investigation. And besides, why must the Christian accept a
Marxist socialist program of revolution and reconstruction as
the only means by which the redemption of the social-political
order could take place? We have witnessed with approval, the
developments of theologies of hope, revolution and liberation,
under some Marxist inspiration. We have learned from them

our own inherent Christian responsibilities in the social and political orders. But we have also noted that certain important problems remain unresolved: violence in revolution, for example. We must in addition acknowledge that while Christian life has an important political dimension, it should not be reduced simply to political activism and political theology.

In his humility and openness to learn from both Marxism and China, the Christian may run another risk: being uncritical of the problems posed by Marxism and the success of the Chinese revolution. The powerful Marxist states, including China, practice a rigid control of intellectual and cultural activities and of the education of the young reminiscent of the dogmatic control exercised by the medieval Church and the post-Reformation churches. Will the Christian oppose such control only on the ground of the inherent opposition to Christianity, or for broader and more human reasons? Should the Christian be satisfied with a double standard of evaluation: that of negating the importance of intellectual and spiritual freedom for socialist humans, while jealously defending the rights of Westerners to criticize their own social and religious establishments? For the Western Christian in particular, an excessive concern to find theological implications in the Chinese experience of the last twenty-five years or so will have real pitfalls. For the person who has not shared in the Chinese experience itself—not even from the outside, so to speak—Marxist ideology, itself originally of Western inspiration and containing influences derived from both the Jewish and Christian traditions, can appear the convenient gateway to an understanding of China. One may then overlook all that is uniquely Chinese in Chinese Communism, as one tends to do in the continuum of the entire Chinese historical experience. It is possible then to run the risk of seeing in Marxism a means of interpreting once and for all the Chinese experience, and end up understanding nothing at all, not even oneself.

And this, tragically enough, has been the mistake of generations of missionaries who sought only to understand China through Christian ideas of sin and grace, of salvation and conversion and damnation.

It is interesting to recall that the eighteenth-century *philo-*

sophies of the European enlightenment had found in the old Chinese civilization reasons for criticizing Christian dogmas and a social order that exalted faith over reason. Today, a new Chinese social order has taken root, finding its inspiration in some of the very ideas nourished earlier by the Enlightenment thinkers and formulated afterward by Feuerbach, Marx and Engels, and decreed as official ideology by Lenin, Stalin and Mao. This new China is posing a symbolic challenge to some of the very foundations of Christian beliefs. Is the Christian God relevant to human life, especially life in a socialist society? Is the only human liberation that from a feudal and bourgeois-capitalist class society, or is there also a higher liberation, not entirely coextensive with the social order? Are the institutional Church and public worship necessary for the continuance of the Christian religion, or could a greater measure of structural de-institutionalization contribute to a more authentic religious life? On the more practical level too, should China ever open its doors again to bearers of the Christian message, will that message be the same again? How can one develop a Chinese theology, when Christians in China have been living in isolation from one another and from the universal Church, while Chinese Christians outside of the People's Republic make up such a small part of a diaspora spread out over all five continents? How can such efforts be fruitful, given also the present stagnation in Christian ecumenism? I voice these problems, not to appear as a prophet of doom, but to highlight the importance of the China question for Christianity itself.

Christianity needs to answer the question of how it can help every human being to become more fully human, individually as well as socially. And the challenge posed by the Chinese experience, whether to eighteenth-century Europe or to today's Catholic Church, is basically a challenge regarding man's humanization. The authenticity of the Chinese claim of liberating man depends upon this criterion. The validity and relevance of the Christian claim must rest upon the same ground. It seems to me that dialogue does not require the other partner to accept one's own vocabulary or philosophical categories, but rather, that both partners should use a *common* language, for example, one based on common *human* values rather than what must be called *Christian* values.

The Chinese belief in human perfectibility is such that teachings about attaining wisdom have always been more important than any concerned with human weakness and wickedness. In Christian vocabulary, the Chinese have always been more preoccupied with a longing for human perfection through self-transcendence and self-forgetfulness, rather than with deliverance from sin. And, except for the influence of Buddhism, the Chinese have always accepted the world and this life as both real and good. For this reason, the next life is given less importance, although it is usually accepted if only by implication—as earlier in the ancestral cult—while a greater importance is given to the *continuance* of this life and this world, as through one's progeny or through one's heroic action, as indicated in the parable of the Foolish Old Man and in the novels of heroic emulation.

Now it is a similar optimism in people that Christianity seeks to express, by a new interpretation of the Genesis story and its relevance for human existence, *Eritis sicut Deus*. This has a positive meaning as well, and need not be understood exclusively in the sense of men and women usurping God's place.

NOTES

1. *Selected Works of Mao Tse-tung* (Peking, 1965), v.2, 305-6 (Taken from "The Chinese Revolution and the Chinese Communist Party," a textbook written jointly by Mao and several other comrades in Yenan, December, 1939).

2. For the Jesuit missions in China, see George H. Dunne, S.J., *Generations of Giants* (University of Notre Dame Press, 1962). For modern missions, see K. S. Latourette, *Christianity in a Revolutionary Age* (London, 1962), v.5.

3. Donald E. MacInnis, *Religious Policy and Practice in Communist China* (New York, 1972), 60.

4. Stuart R. Schram, *The Political Thought of Mao Tse-tung* (New York, 1969), 171-72.

5. MacInnis, op.cit., 12.

6. *Ibid.,* 15.

7. *Ibid.,* 15-16.

8. *Ibid.,* 16.

9. Schram, op.cit., 132-35.

10. Jerome Ch'en, *Mao and the Chinese Revolution* (Oxford, 1965), 185-200.

11. Thomas Berry, "Mao Tse-tung: the Long March" *Theological Implications of the New China* (Geneva & Brussels, 1974), 55-70.

12. Schram, op.cit., 135-6.

13. Julia Ching, "The Christian Way and the Chinese Wall" *America* (November, 1974), 275-78.

14. Schram, op.cit., 139.

15. "Some Reports on China by Fides News Service" in *The Christian Faith and the Chinese Experience* (Geneva & Brussels, 1974), 124-25.

16. Joseph Needham, "A Christian Perspective on the Chinese Experience" in *Anticipation* (Geneva, World Council of Churches, August, 1973), 24-29, *passim.* Let me add here my deep respect for Needham's scholarship and his work on the many volumes of *Science and Civilization in China* (Cambridge University Press).

17. I think here especially of the thesis of Ernst Bloch as expressed in *Atheismus im Christentum* (Frankfurt im M., 1968). Bloch regards man's divinization in the historical process as rendering God obsolete.

Is Maoism Open
to the Transcendent?

PAUL RULE

It has become a commonplace of visitors to China and
Western residents in the People's Republic to describe their
experiences in religious terms. I am not thinking so much of
the pilgrimage of Western Maoists to the Mecca or New Jerusalem of their beliefs and dreams, but of the ordinary uncom-
mitted, or even ideologically hostile observer. For those with
a religious upbringing it seems to evoke irresistibly memories
of a strict religious education, the inculcation of moral taboos,
personal and public devotional practices, the single-mindedness
of a total world view. I have observed this reaction in visitors
of a wide variety of Christian denominational backgrounds,
but especially evangelical Christians and Roman Catholics.
In my own first experience of China in May 1975, after some
ten years of professional engagement with China past and present, as a student and teacher of Chinese history, I was also
somewhat surprised to find a similar reaction.

I say surprised because I have read more than enough of
the writings of Mao Tse-tung and other leading Chinese Communists to be aware of their deep commitment to Marxism, to
dialectical materialism, and seen enough, admittedly from outside, through a glass darkly, to beware of facile judgments
about the complex reality of the life of the quarter of mankind
who inhabit China. On the other hand, I had been engaged
recently in teaching a course on history of religions with special
emphasis on Chinese religion, attempting to assess the peculiar
features of Chinese religiosity, past and present. I was sensitised
to the this-worldly facade that the traditional Chinese value system presents to the neat-minded Westerner with his reli-

gious/secular, church/state, sacred/profane distinctions. Chinese religion has always resisted the categories of the Western observer. From Marco Polo to the Jesuit missionaries, to later diplomats and merchants, it has always been a puzzle. The Jesuit reports of the sixteenth century to the eighteenth century, with which I am most familiar, were shot through with ambiguities. The Chinese were, to the Jesuits, both the most religious and the least religious of people. On the one hand, their whole world was underpinned by "religious" or ultimate values, all of a piece, all deriving ultimately from a transcendent Heaven *(t'ien)*. On the other hand, many Chinese, especially the upper-class, seemed singularly indifferent to devotional religion and theological dogma. The successive European images of the Chinese, Bayle's atheists, Voltaire's deists, the nineteenth-century idolators and pagans, that derived mostly from the reports of the Jesuits and their successors, were equally contradictory and ambiguous.

But, once in China, plunged into the realities of the post-Cultural Revolution order, I was overwhelmed by the "religious" atmosphere. It manifested itself in externals—the slogans, posters, cult images of Maoism—and in the attitudes and behavior of the people we met. It was like living in the world's biggest religious novitiate, and I do not mean this in the pejorative terms of the popular image of religious orders, of joyless, anti-human, external conformity, but in the sense of deep personal commitment, of joy in self-giving, of self-discipline for the sake of higher values.

What follows is a highly personal and rather unscientific attempt at reflection on that experience. It does not pretend to be either theological, or sinological in the strict sense. Many of my comments are necessarily tentative and require further documentation and argument. If they have any coherent viewpoint it is that of an historian of religion who has recognized a new religion to be assimilated and analyzed within the framework of his discipline.[1]

A comprehensive treatment of the subject of Maoism as a religion would demand engaging in the popular and ever inconclusive language-game known as "the definition of religion."

It is bedevilled, not only by philosophical[2] and theological[3] controversy, but also by disagreement among historians and phenomenologists of religion as to the essential and non-essential characteristics of religion. My position, in the main, is to adopt an operational common-sense typology based on an analysis of a wide-ranging sample of phenomena commonly accepted as "religions." However, I would lay more stress than most on the necessity for reference to a transcendent order of reality as the ultimate criterion in borderline cases. As will be seen below, this assumes critical importance in the case of Maoism.

One obvious starting-point for an investigation of the "religion" of contemporary China is the writings and sayings of the leader of the putative religion, the prophet or high-priest of Maoism, Chairman Mao Tse-tung himself. Here we come upon a curious phenomenon. In his formal writings, Mao has very little to say about religion as such. It would seem that he has accepted, since his formative years, that the debate about religion is decided in the negative. Yet, in his less formal pronouncements, especially in recent years, there has been a tendency for the old man to employ religious language, especially in self-assessment. Perhaps this is simply one aspect of the sardonic sense of humor that seems to mark the off-the-record comments of the Chairman. Assured of his unshakeable position, aware of the awe and reverence attached to his every utterance, he seems to delight in using earthy and shocking expressions.[4] But, since some importance has been placed on these remarks, we should first of all look at a sample of them.

Perhaps the most notorious is Mao's remark to Edgar Snow in January 1965 that before long he must see God.[5] For "God," he used the most ancient term for the High God of Chinese tradition, *Shang-ti*.[6] His immediate disavowal seems to indicate that he was using the term ironically, but even there his words are not unambiguous. According to Snow:

> He said again that he was getting ready to see God very soon. Did I believe it?
> "I wonder if you mean you are going to find out whether there is a God. Do you believe *that?*"

No, he did not, but some people who claimed to be well-informed said there was a God.[7]

And then, characteristically, he turned the conversation to politics by pointing out that the gods have often been invoked by both sides in a war or class struggle.

That such remarks are not reserved for foreigners is shown by a similar comment, "When I go to see God. . . ," in a talk at the Central Work Conference, October 25, 1966.[8] Even more amusing is an earlier reference in 1959, to "when the time comes for me to see Marx. . . ."[9] That his intention is ironic is confirmed by a 1956 reference to counter-revolutionaries who will not have time to change before they are summoned by the King of Hell.[10]

Such references are not even confined to off-the-record speeches. One of the "Three Most-Read Articles" of the Cultural Revolution of the late 1960s is "The Foolish Old Man who removed the Mountains" in which God *(Shang-ti)* sends two "angels" to remove the mountains.[11] But Mao's gloss on the traditional story gives it an orthodox Marxist moral.

> Today, two big mountains lie like a dead weight on the Chinese people. One is imperialism, the other is feudalism. The Chinese Communist Party has long made up its mind to dig them up. We must persevere and work unceasingly, and we, too, will touch God's heart. Our God is no other than the masses of the Chinese people. If they stand up and dig together with us, why can't these two mountains be cleared away?[12]

Again, in a talk during his tour of the provinces in 1971, he took up the same theme:

> (Lenin, he says, tells us) that slaves should arise and struggle for truth. There never has been any supreme savior, nor can we rely on gods or emperors. We rely entirely on ourselves for our salvation. Who has created the world of men? We the laboring masses.[13]

For Mao Tse-tung, then, the masses are his god; they create the world; in them lies salvation.

However, I think that we cannot leave the question there. Why should Mao so readily use the language of traditional religion to describe his life's work and exhort the Chinese people to emulation? Why is it not found a jarring note by an audience largely brought up in the new China of scientific materialism? At the very least it suggests a conscious attempt to present Maoism as a substitute-religion, fulfilling the religious needs of the Chinese people. And, perhaps, it indicates something more. This is what we must now examine, by applying the typology of religion to the values and activities of the new China.

Let us begin with the external manifestations of the new religion—the social and personal rituals of Maoism. All of us have seen films of the Tien-an Men Square rallies during the Great Proletarian Cultural Revolution. They have been likened to the meticulously stage-managed Nuremberg rallies of Nazi Germany. But I feel that the culmination of a religious pilgrimage is a better analogy, a Fatima, or a Holy Year ceremony in St. Peter's Square. The Little Red Guards had come, often on foot, often from very large distances, to meet Chairman Mao, to hear him speak, to wave their Little Red Books, and sing their hymns of praise. It is still remembered by many as the great event of their lives. In kindergartens and primary schools, too, a thousand miles from Peking, I have heard Chinese children sing of their ambition to go to Peking to see Chairman Mao, with what seems to be much more than feigned or practiced fervor.

In what sense was the Little Red Book the sacred scripture or Bible of China? (I use the past tense because in the post-Cultural Revolution settlement with its de-emphasization of the innovations of the high-priest of the movement, Lin Piao, the Little Red Book has lost its key significance.) Perhaps it would be a more fruitful analogy to regard the Little Red Book as a catechism, a summary of doctrine for all, and the four volumes of *Selected Works of Mao Tse-tung* as the theological summa of the true faith. In either case, there is no question of the reverence for the Word. It is recited, religiously, on formal oc-

casions; cited as the ultimate authority; sung and repeated end-
lessly in radio broadcasts and over public address systems. It is
comparatively easy to find traditional parallels or prototypes
for this repetitive promulgation of moral and political orthodoxy, for example, the Sacred Edicts of the Ch'ing Emperors,[14]
or the primers for budding literati, like the *San Tzu Ching* or
"Three Character Classic." What is different is the direct appeal to all, even the peasant, and the comprehensiveness of the
teaching. There may be something of the self-interested appeal
to public order of the earlier examples, but there is a deeper
note of claims to absolute truth. Confucius never completely
subdued his rivals and other, alternative "ways" remained real
options. Now there is only Mao.

The Western observer is necessarily skeptical about some
of the claims made for the Little Red Book and the thoughts of
Mao Tse-tung. Was it really the direct inspiration for victories
in ping-pong, engineering marvels, medical miracles, production
increases? Almost invariably, the "thought" of the Chairman
alleged to have produced the result seems to us banal, tautologi-
cal, moralistic. Yet, perhaps we are asking the wrong questions,
assuming that the inspiration for technical innovation should be
technological, that "expertness" rather than "redness" should
prevail, to use the Chinese terminology. A close examination of
the cases nearly always reveals that there is no question of fundamental invention, but of development, application or, again
to use the Marxist cant term, practice. The results are the fruits
of enthusiasm, drive, perseverance: just the results that come
primarily from the will rather than the intellect. How much
human energy is wasted in the West through lack of incentive
and denial of initiative? How many discoveries of our much
vaunted "pure" science are never followed up, developed or
applied? It is not just a question of relevance or utilitarianism.
It is rather a matter of human dignity and ultimate values.

But is it, in the end, religious? And, if religious, is it philosophically and theologically sound? Let us leave aside, for the
moment, questions of essence and ultimacy, and pursue the line
of functional analogy. Do the quotations from Chairman Mao
function in China in the way that scriptural tags or theological

axioms function within Christiaity? Certainly, the analogies with popular religion in the West are striking. Articles in the *People's Daily* or *Red Flag* are redolent of popular preaching. We find the text for the day; the heroic example; the application to daily life; the exhortation; the appeals to shame, fear and group solidarity. The emphasis which, at first, may appear moralistic, i.e., to be aimed at external conformity, emerges as something much closer to St. Ignatius Loyola's emphasis in his *Spiritual Exercises* on "understanding and savoring the matter interiorly." It is not enough to do the right thing, nor even to understand correctly, but to make it part of oneself.

Some misgivings, nevertheless, remain. Is there any freedom of interpretation? The Chinese attitude to the Word is much closer to the Catholic than the Protestant hermeneutical stereotype. In cases of doubt, an authorized interpretation is sought. During the Cultural Revolution rival groups (sects?) ransacked the treasury of Mao's writings in order to find appropriate quotations to justify their opposed lines. Controversy was stilled only when the Chairman himself provided an authoritarian interpretation of his words, and himself selected the operative phrases. The rest were, to use the now famous words of President Nixon's press secretary, "not operative."

Another ground on which this conception of the authoritarian and all conquering "Thoughts of Chairman Mao" may be questioned is apparent assumption of the unlimited perfectibility of man. I will leave the theologians to debate the meaning and implications of original sin and concentrate on a critique from the humanistic point of view. Mao appears to be convinced that a genuinely new man can be created in China, who will be free from all taint of the old bourgeois society. The convulsions of the Cultural Revolution can be, partly at least, explained in terms of this belief which probably has its roots as much in Confucius as in the European Enlightenment.[15] Remnants of old thinking remained even, perhaps especially, within the ranks of the Chinese Communist Party. Mao does not go as far as the *ecclesia semper reformanda* position of Christianity mainly, I suspect, because there is no eschatological dimension, no ideal other-worldly Church or Kingdom to serve as prototype. If the Kingdom is to be realized, it must be of this world. How, then, to explain the patent non-realisation of the Communist Utopia after a generation? Mao never, to my knowledge, seeks a solution in 'liberal' theories of human nature.[16] Failure must come from deficiencies in the social organization and, above all, the education system of the new China. It is the persistence of bourgeois liberal values that prevents the development of true proletarian consciousness.

What rescues Maoism from unreality and question-begging and provides an explanation for the persistence of struggle and tension in society, is Mao's theory of "non-antagonistic contradictions." Although first enunciated in his essay *On Contradiction* (1937) it reached its fullest development during the first serious testing of Mao's faith in human perfectibility, the aftermath of the Hundred Flowers campaign of 1956-1957. In his speech "On the Current Handling of Contradictions among the People" (February 27, 1957), he conceded that, even within the working class and peasantry, in the heart of socialist society, there may lurk contradictions which will lead to disturbance, struggle, tension; not, however, to revolutionary change of government.

> Contradictions in a socialist society are fundamentally different from contradictions in old societies, such as capitalist society. Contradictions in capitalist society find expression in acute antagonisms and conflicts, in sharp class struggle, which cannot be resolved by the capitalist system itself, but only by socialist revolution. But contradictions in socialist society are not antagonistic and can be resolved one after the other by the socialist system itself.[17]

The "non-antagonistic" nature of these contradictions was, one immediately notes, not very evident during the struggles of the late 1960s. It is impossible to regard all the physical and moral victims of the Cultural Revolution as class enemies, and their treatment went far beyond the bounds of Mao's theories. For a time "to rebel is justified" assumed the force of an absolute. But even here, Mao's trust in the revolutionary instincts of the young, in the purity of uncontaminated human nature, is strongly evident.

The trust was, of course, reciprocated. During the Cultural Revolution the cult of Chairman Mao reached extremes, extremes that again inevitably suggest religious analogies. The iconography and symbolism of the Mao cult are subjects that deserve separate and expert study in themselves. But even a brief glance at some of the main symbols suffices to demonstrate that we have more than a leader-cult. Mao was hailed, at the height of the Cultural Revolution, as "our great teacher, great leader, great supreme commander and great helmsman." It might be objected that this is the language of the personality cult of all modern charismatic political leaders—of Mussolini, Hitler, Stalin, Sukarno, Nkrumah, Idi Amin. We are all familiar with the giant statues and portraits of the Leader, the birthday celebrations, the banners and rallies. Writing, as I do, in the middle of an Australian election campaign, I have to admit that there are features of such a cult in Western democracies too. But Mao Tse-tung is not only Leader, in many metaphorical guises, but "the red, red sun in the hearts of the people." I think this metaphor is most revealing. Mao's image not only broods over the Chinese people like some latter-day Buddha, he is *in* the hearts of men, their innermost being, their source of life and energy. Nor, be it noted for later reference, is he a transcendent being, above and remote, like the heaven *(t'ien)* of Chinese tradition; nor is his mandate communicated by bureaucratic intermediaries as in the mandate of heaven doctrine of Imperial China. He provides immediate and direct personal access.

Does this, in the end, amount to a religious cult in any more than an extended analogical sense? Frederic Wakeman, whose analysis of the "Red Sun" metaphor is extremely perceptive, seems to me to get the cult of Mao almost exactly wrong when he says:

> To say "the cult of Mao" is to risk melding usages, so that the term sounds deprecatory, implying superstitious idolatry. Yet, like a purely religious cult, the veneration of Mao does help secure a theodicy in the form of a person. But

Mao, however charismatic, has been no exemplary prophet: his cult, though liturgical, distinctly lacks ritual specificity.[18]

Elsewhere in the same chapter of his *History and Will*,[19] he
rightly points to the lack of distinction between religious and
secular spheres in Maoism, and, he might well have added, in
Chinese thought in general. But the conclusion is surely not that
the Mao-cult is therefore a theodicy, either in the classical Leib-
nizian sense, or in a wider sense that some sort of God is manifested or his existence demonstrated in the person of Mao Tse-
tung. Mao is precisely a prophet, a mouthpiece for the forces of
history. It is in his thought, or perhaps, more accurately in
Chinese, his "thinking" *(ssu-hsiang);* an ongoing process of
reading the signs of the times, moulding political practice to the
contours of socio-economic reality, that is his contribution to
Chinese Marxism. He does not initiate a doctrine, an '-ism'[20]
(chu-i in Chinese, as in *Ma-k'o-ssu chu-i,* 'Marxism') but applies it to Chinese conditions. It is precisely "specificity" that is
his contribution to Marxism, and the rituals reinforce this sini-
fied doctrine. Hence the liturgical trappings of a public room in
China: the portraits of the four founders—Marx, Engels, Lenin,
Stalin—and separate and often larger, because more important
to China, Mao Tse-tung. It is not a cult of Mao, but of
Maoism, the thoughts of Mao Tse-tung, and Mao is honored as
the thinker of the thoughts. Once more we are forced back onto
the content and scope of the doctrine to answer our question.

Most religions have a distinctive code of ethics, and
Maoism is no exception. It is often labelled "Puritanism" and,
in the popular sense of that term, it is so, namely a doctrine of
hard work, strict sexual and personal behavior, unselfishness
and egalitarianism. Admittedly the system rewards such behavior by the material rewards of status and salary, but I have seen
no concrete evidence that it is treated in a cynical or opportunist
fashion by most Chinese. The reward of "cadre" statues is a du-
bious privilege, especially in post-Cultural Revolution China. It
involves the recipient in many gratuitous and demanding
tasks, such as working without salary on national days and holi-
days, extended political education sessions, and now, processing

in a May Seventh Cadre School. The combination of physical labor and intensive ideological training that we saw in the main Shanghai Cadre School is a daunting regime indeed. And the fate of so many bureaucrats during the 1960s, and earlier, points to the ease of "falling from grace." The punishment for dereliction, more usually moral pressure than physical, no doubt is important in maintaining the ethic, as it was in Puritan England or Calvin's Geneva. But the cheerful unselfishness of the young especially, is refreshing and could hardly be feigned for visitors. It is this cheerful enthusiasm and its constant reference to a doctrinal source, that mark it off as a religious ethic. It is inner-directed, not imposed from outside. And its aim is service of others, not self-fulfillment. It has an ecstatic quality that firmly places it within the parameters of the conventional definitions of religion.[21]

The social functions of religious systems as delineated by sociologists—legitimation, consolation, orientation—are abundantly fulfilled by Maoism. This is true not only in the broad terms of Peter Berger[22] and others where, by definition, the value system that performs such functions is a religion of the society concerned. Even in the narrower framework of analysis of classical sociology of religion, Maoism appears to perform strictly religious functions. It contains the ultimate answers to questions about the meaning and purpose of life, the significance of death, the hierarchy of social and personal values. It legitimates the social order by, for example, the concept of the dictatorship of the proletariat, which is the focus of the current study campaign in China. Once more, however, it goes beyond mere political legitimation to fundamental questions of man's mastery over nature, what has often been called the Promethean strain in Chinese communism.[23] "Learn from Tachai," the model commune literally carved out of the Shansi hills, means far more than to imitate their techniques of terracing and water articulation. It is an exhortation to conquer the earth in the spirit of the revolution and the thoughts of Chairman Mao. The heroes and martyrs of the revolution (some of them suspect, shades of Christian hagiography) are lauded for placing service of the masses before life itself.

Another strain in Maoism with strong religious overtones

is that of "conversion." The process of struggle, criticism, transformation has many likenesses to evangelical conversion and to Catholic repentance, confession and reparation. To generalize boldly on the basis of the literature of thought reform,[24] one is struck by the emphasis on what a Christian might call *metanoia,* change of heart. It is rectification of ideas and lifestyle rather than mere external conformity that is sought. And, characteristically, and in stark contrast to the Soviet Russian techniques of social control, the techniques employed aim at transforming not breaking the individual. In a sense, it is "brain-washing," and the methods of alternating fear and inducement, group pressure and isolation, evolving "confessions" and study of the thoughts of Chairman Mao, are psychologically sophisticated and extraordinarily effective. Undoubtedly, it is a painful experience, but the aim, if not always the result, is to enable the individual to choose reality, to liberate himself from illusion. An unnamed Catholic diplomat in China, quoted by Maria Macciocchi, seems to me to catch the spirit of the process well:

As for Chinese intellectuals, my feelings on the subject of their re-education and self-criticism are quite different from the conventional Western view. Those who really understand China realize that these experiences are not as painful as they are made out to be, but rather a sort of liberation of the individual. Re-educating yourself means becoming part of the masses again and part of the mass religion. Inner freedom, happiness, and a sense of spirituality are achieved by being re-educated among the ordinary people, peasants and workers, since the ultimate humiliation in life is to be isolated from the masses. . . . The day when (the intellectual) is accepted again, like the prodigal son, is a day of reconciliation for him.

You have heard of self-criticism. I have not had this happen to me, but I know that self-criticisms in China are made and then remade many times over like a work of art. The man or woman who undergoes this experience has to be completely sincere because he or she has to speak out loud in public. This public loves this person and wants to redeem him, and it exposes his limitations, his weaknesses, and any hypocritical attitudes he may unknowingly have had. When the self-criticism has fully satisfied the masses, the person in question has achieved a sort of absolute sublimation of the self.[25]

Some severe reservations must remain as to the cost in human terms of such methods. They are open, like all religious practices, to the abuses of hypocrisy, playing the system and moral coercion. It might also be argued that "conversion" is a much more effective means of social control than force, and may, therefore, be employed in a cynical spirit by the masters of the new China. Yet the cynicism may be on our part, too, as shown by our unwillingness to accept the expressions, and more importantly, the actions, of our Chinese contemporaries as genuine and freely chosen. Whatever our ultimate judgment, at least the functional analogy with religion holds up. Like all major world religions, Maoism claims the whole person.

The great doubt that remains in my mind about Maoism as a religion is the ultimate frame of reference, the acknowledgment of, or even possibility of, transcendence within the system. Transcendence is an ambiguous term, deliberately so in order to avoid specifying and characterizing the transcendent object. As a concept in the phenomenology of religion, it avoids problems raised by specific theistic terminology. It allows Theravada Buddhism, for example, and later Confucianism, to be unequivocally ranked as religions, despite difficulties in identifying a God-concept. On the other hand, it is notoriously difficult to define satisfactorily without lapsing back into the dilemmas which led to its use.[26] Clearly, it is in origin metaphorical and implies a belief in an order of existence beyond immediate and ordinary experience or consciousness. I would go further, and argue that it demands going beyond the bounds of the material, and that in accepting the existence of the non-material is implied the existence of transcendent being, i.e., in more traditional language, of God.[27]

Ninian Smart, whose analysis of Maoism as a religion I

have largely accepted up to this point, balks at the concept of transcendence.

> It is true that typically religions involve reference to the transcendent or supernatural, and yet Mao's doctrines are this-worldly. Still, there is a certain transcendence of the empirical in the flavor of his teachings.[28]

But, where precisely is this "certain transcendence of the empirical" to be found? Not, surely, in any belief in another world or another realm of reality, despite such playful allusions as those in Mao's poem *The Immortals*.[29] Certainly, Mao preaches the transcendence of egotism and individual self-seeking, the losing of oneself in the masses. There is also a strong element of transcendence of the present, a future hope.[30] However, in the end, his hope rests in the masses and their material well-being.

Yet, for all Mao's professional materialism, Smart is right in pointing to "a certain transcendence of the empirical in the flavor of his teachings." There is an emphasis on spirituality—reflection, self-examination, consciousness, integrity—that we would spontaneously interpret as incompatible with dialectical materialism, at least in its grosser Soviet form. The Chinese Communists, especially in the Cultural Revolution, seemed to be reaching toward an understanding of human action that would exalt the human will and understanding above the limitations of matter that would, in Marxist terms, make superstructure independent of base. Here, for example, is the *People's Daily* for May 28, 1966:

> About the relation of spirit and matter (one must say) that matter is primary and spirit is secondary. But this is said only about the genesis of thought, when matter comes first, then spirit. It is not true about the strength of the two. The strength of spirit is much greater than that of matter. . . . Once the masses seize the correct thoughts of the advanced class, then this becomes a great material force. . . . Therefore we must pay great attention to ideological work. The Thoughts of Mao Tse-tung is the sun in our heart, is the root of our life, is the source of all our strength. Through

this, man becomes unselfish, daring, intelligent, able to do everything; he is not conquered by any difficulty and can conquer every enemy. The Thoughts of Mao Tse-tung transforms man's ideology, transforms the Fatherland. . . . Through this the oppressed people of the world will rise.[31]

This strain of voluntaryism, of "revolutionary romanticism"[32] is very strong in Mao's writings, and even stronger in his tactics and leadership. It is open to divergent interpretation. Some would see it as a source of contradiction between his explicit ideology, his materialism, and his practice. Others would see it as part of his Chineseness: the legacy of Confucian moralism[33] and the Chinese peasant rebellion tradition. Others, again, have seen it as a psychological device, using the rhetoric of "immortality" to arouse the consciousness of the masses. The psychiatrist, Robert Jay Lifton, seems to be arguing the last case,[34] although he is ambiguous as to whether it is a conscious ploy on Mao's part, or springing from the depths of his complex personality.[35] Focusing on the Cultural Revolution, he writes:

Much of what has been taking place in China recently can be understood as a quest for revolutionary immortality. By revolutionary immortality I mean a shared sense of participating in permanent revolutionary fermentation, and of transcending individual death by "living on" indefinitely within this continuing revolution.[36]

Later, he insists that Mao has always associated the revolutionary's attitude toward death with "a mode of transcendence."[37] But is it a "mode," an ontological reality, or a rhetorical device? Just as Smart imputes "transcendence" to "the flavor" of Mao's teaching, so, ultimately, Lifton appears to regard it as belonging to the communication, not the substance of Maoism:

Underneath the assumption of oppression being worse than death is a characteristically Maoist *tone of transcendence,* a message to the revolutionary which seems to say that death does not really exist for him; he has absolutely nothing to fear.[38]

Nevertheless, it is such a constant theme in Mao's writings and actions, so consonant with his revolutionary experiences such as the 1927 debacle, the Long March, and the Anti-Japanese War, that I do not believe it is purely rhetorical or tactical. Outside the framework of Marxist orthodoxy it may be, but nonetheless authentically Maoist for that.

How then to assess Maoism as a religion? The method of functional analogy has revealed many "religious" features of Maoism, but left open the question of functional substitution. Perhaps Maoism is a substitute-religion, deliberately usurping the traditional religious ground. The attempt to apply an ultimate criterion, that of transcendence, has revealed an aspect of transcendence but one that is ambivalent and inconclusive. The New China is certainly overtly anti-religious in its policy toward traditional Chinese and foreign religions. Yet again, paradoxically, this very inability to tolerate rivals may be evidence of Maoism's ambitions to be the one, true faith of China. It leaves no room for rivals precisely because it ambitions to occupy fully all spheres of human activity including that we call religion. If it is not a religion, it looks remarkably like one. It was Confucius who insisted that names should correspond to realities and realities to names. I believe that there is enough of the reality of "religion" to Maoism to merit the title, and that avoidance of it may blind us to vital aspects of its hold on the Chinese people.

To conclude that Maoism should be called a religion may appear a purely speculative, academic judgment without practical implications. For those interested in the future of Christianity in China, however, it seems to be laden with significance. I do not regard it as giving comfort along the lines that the Chinese are not as irreligious as they seem. On the contrary, I think that the very religiousness of Maoism will make it more, not less, impervious to the Christian message. It also implies that any future approach to the conversion of China will have to be through, not outside of, the concepts, language and sociology of Maoism, at least in the near future. The missionary to the New China will be preaching not to atheists but to believers in the religion of Mao Tse-tung.

NOTES

1. The only attempt I know of to consider Maoism in this perspective is the recent work by Professor Ninian Smart of the Lancaster University Department of Religious Studies, *Mao*, London, 1974.

2. E.g., the empiricist's insistence on empirical verificability as a criterion for meaningfulness in religious language.

3. Especially on the part of the disciples of Karl Barth and Dietrich Bonhoeffer who, for different reasons, wish to place Christianity outside the sphere of "religion."

4. This is evident in many of the comments recorded in collections such as Stuart Schram's *Mao Tse-tung Unrehearsed* (Harmondsworth, 1974). Mao in conversation appears to indulge in ribaldry, dialect jokes and wisecracks.

5. E. Snow, *The Long Revolution* (New York, 1973) p. 219.

6. His actual words, in Chinese, were: *pu chiu yao chien Shang-ti, ibid.*

7. *Ibid.*, p. 220.

8. S. Schram, Ed., *Mao Tse-tung Unrehearsed*, p. 220.

9. *Ibid.*, p. 154, from a speech of September 11, 1959.

10. *Ibid.*, p. 76, from "On the Ten Great Relationships."

11. Mao Tse-tung, *Selected Works*, III (Peking, 1965) p. 322. The "angels" of the authorized English translation are in the original *shen*, "spirits" *Mao Tse-tung hsuan chi* (Peking, 1966) p. 1102.

12. *Ibid.*

13. Schram, *Mao Tse-tung Unrehearsed*, p. 297.

14. See John Israel, "Continuities and Discontinuities in the Ideology of the Great Proletarian Cultural Revolution," in C. Johnson, Ed., *Ideology and Politics in Contemporary China* (Seattle, 1973) especially p. 29.

15. Frederic Wakeman in *History and Will: Philosophical Perspectives of Mao Tse-tung's Thought* (Berkeley, 1973) argues strongly for enlightenment influence on Mao via Kant and the late nineteenth-century Chinese reformers. In this respect, however, I find much more convincing John Passmore's argument in *The Perfectibility of Man* (New York, 1970) for the precedence in time and influence of Confucius. See especially a long note on p. 160.

16. In his "Talks at the Yenan Forum on Art and Literature" (1942) he insists that "there is only human nature of a class character" not in the abstract (Selected Works, III, Peking, 1965) p. 90.

17. S. Schram, Ed., *The Political Thought of Mao Tse-tung* (New York, 1963) pp. 239-240.

18. F. Wakeman, *History and Will,* (Berkeley, 1973) p. 19, note. He goes on, for the section quoted, to refer this typology to Max Weber's *Sociology of Religion.*

19. Ch. 2, "The Red Sun," especially pp. 19-20.

20. I use the term "Maoism" throughout this essay as a convenient and unavoidable label, without prejudice as to the outcome of the famous argument as to whether there is a Mao-ism (v. *The China Quarterly,* Nos. 1, 2 and 4, 1960). My point here is a purely linguistic one.

21. See, for example, Ch. 1 of Max Weber, *The Sociology of Religion* (London, 1965) especially pp. 1-5.

22. *The Social Reality of Religion* (London, 1969) with its emphasis on world-construction and world-maintenance as the basic functions of religion.

23. Schram, *The Political Thought of Mao Tse-tung,* p. 54.

24. See, for example, R. J. Lifton, *Thought Reform and the Psychology of Totalism,* (New York and London, 1961) and T. Chen, *Thought Reform of the Chinese Intellectuals* (Hong Kong, 1960).

25. M. A. Macciocchi, *Daily Life in Revolutionary China* (New York, 1972) pp. 109-110.

26. See, for example, Alistair Kee's *The Way of Transcendence: Christian Faith without Belief in God* (Harmondsworth, 1971) in which the author carefully avoids defining the concept of "transcendence" which will, he believes, enable him to perform the *tour de force* of eliminating *theos* from theology.

27. Without developing this further here, I would refer the reader to Ch. XIX, "General Transcendent Knowledge" of Bernard Lonergan's *Insight* (London, 1957).

28. *Mao,* p. 84.

29. In which Mao places his dead wife, Yang K'ai-hsu, and old comrade Liu Chih-hsun in the mythical world of the Man and Woman in the moon.

30. This is, of course, the one area where Christian-Marxist dialogue has succeeded in finding a *point d'appui,* especially following the neo-Marxist Ernst Bloch.

31. "Marxism Revised," *China News Analysis,* No. 635, Nov. 4, 1966, p. 7.

32. v. Stuart Schram, *Mao Tse-tung,* Harmondsworth, 1966, pp. 293-294.

33. v. D. Nivison, "Communist Ethics and Chinese Tradition" in *Journal of Asian Studies,* XVI, 1956-7, p. 51ff.

34. *Revolutionary Immortality: Mao Tse-tung and the Chinese Cultural Revolution,* Harmondsworth, 1970.

35. "The revolutionary denies theology as such, but embraces a secular utopia through images closely related to the spiritual conquest of death and even to an afterlife" *Ibid.,* p. 22. What is unclear is whether Lifton regards this use of religious imagery as a conscious "secularization" or appropriation of religious language.

36. *Ibid.,* pp. 20-21.

37. *Ibid.,* pp. 65-66.

38. *Ibid.,* p. 68.

Mao's Thought and Christian Belief

ROBERT FARICY, S.J.

The purpose of this study is not to understand the contemporary Chinese experience, something that could be done only by living that experience. Nor is the purpose primarily to understand Mao Tse-tung's thought. The effort here is to better understand the Christian experience by reacting from a Christian standpoint to the ideology of Mao Tse-tung. "The Chinese experience," writes Julia Ching, "calls upon Christian believers everywhere to probe deeper into their own faith."[1] The point is to make a Christian response to what the Peking Foreign Languages Press calls "Mao Tse-tung thought."

The study has three main parts. First, the basic principles of Mao's ideology are presented. As a first response to these principles, some fundamental Christian doctrines are pointed out, statements that Christian teaching can make to Mao Tse-tung thought. As a second further response to Mao's ideology, some lessons that Christian theology might learn from Mao's thought are considered.

I

MAO TSE-TUNG'S BASIC IDEOLOGY

There are various possible general approaches to Chinese Communism: historical, economic, political, and others. The approach here is to examine briefly the ideology of Chinese Communism, the thought of Mao Tse-tung, so as to see the internal logic and consistency of that ideology. Once this is done,

Mao's thought-system will be looked at "from outside," from a Christian point of view.

By the term "ideology," different people mean different things. Often, the word is used pejoratively, to denote a rigid set of philosophical guidelines that belongs to someone else, usually the "other side." Here, however, "ideology" simply refers to the basic propositions or ideas that are intended to structure the values and attitudes, the culture, of a society. The importance of Chinese Communist ideology is evident. One person in four lives in China; one third of the Third World and two thirds of those people under Communist regimes live in China. It is true, of course, that Mao Tse-tung thought is a Chinese Communist ideal, and that it surely has not been entirely accepted and assimilated by every resident of Communist China. Nevertheless, its influence has been and is enormous, and will continue to be long after the death of Mao. Even if there are, in the future, radical ideological changes in China, it remains true that hundreds of millions of Chinese have been formed, have been trained to think, act, and evaluate, according to Mao's ideology.

What are the basic principles of Mao Tse-tung thought? In Mao's ideology, the idea of a future utopic and conflict-free society does not exist. There is no place for the concept of an ultimate peaceful society which would be the final goal and the end-product of Communist revolution and political development. For Mao, the revolution is continuous. "I stand," Mao writes, "for the theory of permanent revolution."[2] The revolutionary struggle will go on as long as there are men, because struggle is the heart and essence of human reality. In Mao Tse-tung thought, the emphasis is strongly on the principles of revolutionary action. The two main ideas are Mao's concept of struggle, and his understanding of the relationship between theory and practice; these two ideas find further application in his theory of communication.

Struggle and Contradiction

If there is one central idea in Mao's thought, it is that of "contradiction," of the unity and conflict of opposites. Even Mao's idea of the theory-practice relationship is an application of the more fundamental idea of contradiction. The conflicts and contradictions that are found in nature (life-death, dark-light, cold-hot, and so on) that eventually found their way into Hegel's philosophy and later into the materialist dialectics of Marx, Engels, and Lenin, are more important in the Chinese tradition than in the West. Partly perhaps because of the greater importance of the notions of complementarity and of conflict, of the unity of opposites (Ying and Yang) in traditional Chinese culture, the idea of contradiction is more central and more basic in Mao Tse-tung thought than it is for Marx, Engels, or Lenin.[3] For Mao, contradiction is the fundamental principle and the mainspring of all reality and especially of human society; this is true for all society, whether capitalist, socialist, or communist. "Contradiction," here, is a technical term; clearly, it does not refer to the logical contradiction of western medieval philosophy, but rather to the opposition of contraries which have at least enough in common to be in some kind of union.

In a talk in 1956, Mao lists the ten most important contradictions for China to face at that time. They are good examples of what Mao means by contradiction: (1) the relationships between industry and agriculture, and between heavy and light industries; (2) the relationship between coastal industry and the industry of China's interior; (3) the relationship between economic construction and defense construction; (4) the relationships between units of production, producers, and government; (5) the relationship between central and regional authorities; (6) relationships between various ethnic groups; (7) the relationship between revolutionary and counter revolutionary; (8) the relationship between the party and those outside the party; (9) the relationship between right and wrong; (10) the relationships between China and other nations.[4]

Mao presents his political philosophy of contradiction chiefly in two essays, "On Contradiction" (1937), and "On the Correct Handling of Contradiction Among the People" (1957).[5] The first essay begins, "The law of contradiction in things, that is, the law of the unity of opposites, is the basic law of materialist dialectics.''[6] Mao goes on to oppose, in a didactic and over-simplified way, two basic philosophies or, rather, two fundamental ways of viewing reality. He describes the first as a metaphysical worldview, the view that has dominated western capitalist society and that has developed into a "vulgar evolutionist" approach to things. The basic postulates of this worldview are that essences, human nature for instance, are unchanging; that any change is quantitative, not qualitative (for example, a lower form cannot change into a higher); and that change comes about through external forces (through efficient causality). Opposed to this is the worldview of dialectical materialism, which had developed from Hegel's idealist dialectics through the work of Marx, Engels, Lenin, and Stalin, and is the basis for the way the new China understands man, nature, society, and their interrelationships. Whereas the metaphysical or vulgar evolutionist world view sees things as isolated and as static, materialist dialectics

> holds that in order to understand the development of a thing we should study it internally and in its relations with other things; in other words, the development of things should be seen as their internal and necessary self movement, while each thing in its movement is interrelated with and interacts on the things around it. The fundamental cause of the development of a thing is not external but internal; it lies in the contradictoriness within the thing.[7]

Changes in nature are due chiefly to the internal contradictions in nature. Changes in society are caused principally by the contradictions in society. And, since everything has internal contradictions, everything changes. Not only human society changes, but human nature itself is in flux, changing and changeable.[8] Eventually the human race will die out or will be transformed into something else. Even Communism itself, a final stage in traditional Marxism and in Soviet Marxism, will, Mao holds, be in continuous change—in an ongoing state of permanent revolution—and eventually be transformed into something else.[9]

The two world outlooks differ not only in their contents but also in their orientations, in their purpose. The metaphysical view aims at understanding reality for its own sake. Materialist dialectics, on the other hand, "teaches us primarily how to observe and analyze the movements of opposites in different things and, on the basis of such analysis, to indicate the methods for resolving contradictions."[10] Mao's approach to reality is one of the understanding that is ordered to practice, ordered to changing reality by working through and resolving the contradictions.

All development, then, is due to the unity of opposites, the contradiction, that one finds interior to each thing; this is true, for example, for the growth of living bodies and for the progress of society. This does not, of course, eliminate the importance of external causes, which are often the occasions of change. But the basis and the fundamental reason for all change and motion is the contradictions within whatever is changing. "Between the opposites in a contradiction," Mao explains, "there is at once unity and struggle, and it is this that impels things to move and change. Contradictions exist everywhere, but they differ in accordance with the different nature of different things."[11]

This does not mean that every duality or relationship is a contradiction. Many relationships are simply non-contradictory. On the other hand, a previously non-contradictory duality can become a relationship of opposition in unity, a contradiction.

Contradiction, the unity of opposites, is universal; and in the process of the development of each thing a movement of opposites exists from beginning to end.[12] Opposition and struggle, then, form the most fundamental law of reality. This is true, also, of the Chinese Communist Party; opposition and struggle within the party are "a reflection within the party of contradictions between classes and between the new and the old in society; if there were no contradictions in the party and no ideological struggles to resolve them, the party's life would come to an end."[13] Contradiction permeates and makes go every process. In any organism and in any society, stability is not the normal state; what is normal is conflict and change. In a given society, it is not change or conflict that needs to be explained, but stability and consensus. This is just the opposite of the ordinary western approach to society, which assumes stability to be normal and desirable, and which tries to account for change and conflict.[14]

The law of contradiction is more central and more fundamental in Mao's thought than in the philosophy of Marx or the writings of Lenin. Mao is closer to Engels, who describes reality dialectically in terms of three categories: the unity of opposites, the transformation of quantity into quality, and the negation of the negation. However, Mao is more radical than Engels in his conception of the law of contradiction; he reduces all three categories to the basic law of contradiction, to the law of the unity of opposites. For Mao, the transformation of quantity and quality into one another is the unity of the opposites of quantity and quality; it is an instance of the law of contradiction.[15] And the law of negation of the negation, for Mao, does not exist at all. "In the development of things, every link in the chain of events is both affirmation and negation."[16] Slave-holding society, for example, negated primitive society but affirmed feudal society; capitalist society is the negation of feudal society, but it affirms—leads inevitably to—socialist society. That is, slave-holding and feudal societies, feudal and capitalist societies, capitalist and socialist societies—these are all unities of opposites. All development, for Mao, is in the fundamental category of his theory of contradictions.

In analyzing any social situation, one must search for the principal contradiction, or conflict, at the heart of the society in question; for it is that conflict that determines and structures the situation. Secondary contradictions are also to be identified and clearly distinguished from the principal contradiction. Furthermore, the principal and non-principal aspects of these contradictions should be identified and studied. All this may seem abstract; on the contrary, contradictions are always particular, and each must be studied objectively in its own concrete and unique historicity.

In the conflict of opposites that is contradiction, there is also to be found the unity of opposites, and this is their identity with each other. Mao quotes the Chinese proverb, "Things that oppose each other also complement each other."[17] It is true that the contradictory aspects in every process oppose each other, and that pairs of opposed aspects also oppose each other. How can one speak of unity or identity? For one thing, because no contradictory aspect can exist in isolation. "Without life," Mao writes, "there would be no death; without death, there would be no life."[18] Without bad luck, there could be no good luck; without good luck, there would be no bad luck. Without landlords, there would be no tenants; without tenants, no landlords. Without the bourgeoisie, no proletariat; without the proletariat, no bourgeoisie. Without imperialism, no colonies, and vice versa. Each contradictory aspect is the condition for the other's existence. Moreover, under given conditions, each contradictory aspect is transformed into its opposite; ruler becomes ruled, the revolutionary becomes counter-revolutionary, peasants become land-holders. "The oppressor and the oppressed are transformed into one another; . . . . War is transformed into peace, and peace into war."[19] This, then, is the full meaning of the unity of the opposites that form a contradiction: they depend on each other for their existence, and they can be transformed into one another. Materialist dialectics search for the identity in concrete transformations.

The unity of opposites, however, is relative and transitory. But the struggle of opposites is absolute. Note that the only absolute for Mao is struggle, together with the development process that struggle results in. Paradoxically enough, but logically in Mao's ideology, the only absolute is struggle and the development it produces.

At this point, Mao brings up the question of antagonisms. In "On Contradiction," although mentioning the existence of non-antagonistic contradictions, he elaborates chiefly on the antagonistic kind. In the later essay, "On the Correct Handling of Contradictions Among the People," he goes into detail concerning non-antagonistic contradictions. The distinction is an essential one in Mao's ideology. Antagonistic contradictions are those that arise between the people and the enemies of the people. Non-antagonistic contradictions are those that are found among the people. There is a clear distinction and a qualitative difference between the two; in practice, however, one can be mistaken for the other.

Antagonistic contradictions, those between the people and enemies of the people, are resolved only by suppression of the enemies. This suppression may take the form of ruthless purges or even of war. In the context of the struggle to overcome an antagonistic contradiction, violence is often necessary. In one of his poems, Mao glorifies combat:

> In June our soldiers of heaven fight against
>   evil and rot.
> They have a huge rope to tie up the whale
>   or fabulous cockatrice.
> On the far side of the Kan water the
>   ground turns red. . . .[20]

Non-antagonistic contradictions, the kind that arise between two categories of the people (between peasants and industrial workers, for example) can be worked out through honest criticism and open discussion. In these cases, the struggle takes the form of confrontation and cooperation.

The distinction between antagonistic and non-antagonistic contradictions is not always clear, and conflicts must be studied carefully to determine which of the two they are. In the Communist Party, ideological conflicts reflect class contradictions. "At first," Mao writes,

> with regard to certain issues, such contradictions may not manifest themselves as antagonistic. But with the development of class struggle, they may grow and become antagonistic. The history of the Communist Party of the Soviet Union shows us that the contradictions between the correct thinking of Lenin and Stalin and the fallacious thinking of Trotsky, Bukharin, and others did not at first manifest themselves in an antagonistic form, but that later they did develop into antagonism. There are similar cases in the history of the Chinese Communist Party.[21]

Ultimately, whether or not a contradiction is antagonistic depends on who are "the people."

Obviously, it is important to know what constitutes the people, and who the people's enemies are. The boundary between the people and the enemies of the people is flexible; it depends on the attitudes that persons or groups take to the principal social conflict at any given time. The concepts "the people" and "the enemies of the people" are ideological concepts, not sociological, nor economic, nor even primarily political.

Who are the people, the proletariat? For Marx, "proletariat" was an economic concept, for Lenin it was a political concept. But for Mao, "proletariat" is an ideological category. All who are firmly on the side of the party, including merchants and artists and intellectuals, are the proletariat, the people.[22]

What is the purpose and value, within Mao Tse-tung's ideology, of the theory of contradictions? It does not really explain contradiction, nor struggle, nor development. It is, rather, a descriptive theory; it presents and organizes concepts in such a way that they can be used to describe, to study, and to analyze social conflict and change. Mao's theory of contradictions is a way of thinking about reality rather than a way of explaining it. And it is a theory designed for use. The whole point is not so much to know the nature or essence of a contradiction as to identify the principal and the secondary contradictions in a given social situation, and to identify the principal and secondary aspects of a contradiction, precisely so that the contradiction can be resolved. The entire theory is ordered to the resolution of contradictions in the direction of positive social development.

Mao's distinction between antagonistic and non-antagonistic contradictions permits him to affirm that struggle (either antagonistic or non-antagonistic) is at the heart of all social progress. It is for this reason that the revolution is continuous; and it will continue until the death and disappearance of mankind. In 1958, Mao wrote that the law of the unity of opposites —that is, the law of contradiction, of struggle—is absolute and universal. "But," he continues,

the nature of struggle and revolution is different from the past; it is not a class struggle, but a struggle between the

advanced and the backward among the people, a struggle
between advanced and backward science and technology.
The transition from socialism to communism is a struggle,
a revolution. With the advent of the communist era, there
will also be many, many stages of development. . . . All
kinds of mutation and leap are a kind of revolution and
must go through struggle.[23]

Mao's idea of struggle, of the law of the unity of opposites,
is by no means confined to social situations. It is the law of all
reality. "The law of the unity of opposites is the fundamental
law of the universe. This law operates universally, whether in
the natural world, in human society, or in man's thinking."[24]
Mao's teaching on the relationship between practice and theory,
therefore, depends heavily on his theory of contradictions, and
also throws some light on that theory.

Practice and Theory

It is typical of Mao that his classic essay on the practice-
theory relationship is entitled simply "On Practice."[25] For Mao,
practice always has the primacy over theory, and any valid
knowledge or reflection or formulation of thought grows out of
practice and has value only insofar as it is ordered to practice.
Knowledge depends on practice and is for practice. Mao's understanding of the dependence of all theoretical knowledge on
practice, not only for its existence but also for its truth, verification, and value, is an epistemology, a theory of knowing. But it
is more than epistemology; it is also, and more importantly, a
theory of action and a key structural element of Mao's whole
ideology of revolutionary action.

The path to knowledge is direct practical experience. "If
you want to know a certain thing or a certain class of things directly, you must personally participate in the practical struggle
to change reality, to change that thing or class of things. . . . If
you want knowledge, you must take part in the practice of
changing reality."[26] Mao is saying more than simply that direct

knowledge comes from concrete experience. He is also pointing out that the direct experience that results in knowledge changes the reality that is known. "If you want to know the taste of a pear, you must change the pear by eating it yourself."[27] This is not to deny the validity of tradition or of knowledge through indirect experience; most of man's knowledge is, in fact, not based on his own direct contact with what he knows. Nevertheless, ultimately, all genuine knowledge goes back to the direct experience of someone; and so, in one way or another, all valid knowledge is based on direct contact with the concrete reality of what is known. In support, Mao cites the old Chinese proverb, "How can you catch tiger cubs without entering the tiger's lair?"[28]

To be exact, correct ideas come from, and only from, social practice. In "Where Do Correct Ideas Come From?," an essay of 1963, Mao writes that true theoretical knowledge comes from three kinds of social practice: the struggle for production, the class struggle, and scientific experimentation.[29]

To put it another way, all rational knowledge begins in the senses, begins with the perception of concrete objects in the external world.[30] Rational knowledge begins with the experience of perception. The first stage of Mao's philosophy of knowledge, then, is the perception of a particular situation in which one is directly involved. The second stage is the development of this perceptual knowledge into theoretical knowledge; this is a process of reflection, of organizing the data of perception, of the formulation of experience into conceptual knowledge. It is in this way that man comes to understand the laws of the world outside himself.

The third stage of Mao's theory of knowledge is, for him, by far the most important. This is the phase of "applying the knowledge of these laws actively to change the world."[31] Theory, then, is important; without revolutionary theory there can be no revolutionary movement. But the importance of theory consists entirely in that it can guide action. "Theoretical knowledge, which is acquired through practice, must then return to practice."[32] The leap from concrete experience to theoretical knowledge must be complemented by another leap from theory to revolutionary practice. "The knowledge which grasps the laws of the world must be redirected to the practice of changing the world, must be applied anew in the practice of production, in the practice of revolutionary . . . struggle, and in the practice of scientific experiment."[33] This third stage belongs properly to the theory of knowledge because it is the stage of testing, verifying, and developing theoretical knowledge; it is the final phase of the dialectical process of cognition. Does theoretical knowledge correspond to reality? The correspondence to objective facts depends partly on perception, but the truth of the knowledge is verified, and corrected and refined, by putting the knowledge into action. When the theoretical knowledge is redirected to social practice, to what extent does it achieve the goals one has in mind? It is to this extent that the theoretical knowledge is true; to the degree that the knowledge does not work, does not produce the desired results when it is practiced —to that extent the knowledge needs to be revised in the light of its performance. "Practice is the criterion of truth."[34]

It has been pointed out that Mao's pragmatism is not completely foreign to western philosophy, and that it closely parallels the pragmatism of William James and John Dewey.[35] But the parallelism should by no means be overdrawn. Mao's "practice-theory-practice" philosophy of knowledge is far more thoroughgoing, more radical, more *praxis*-oriented, than the philosophies of Dewey and James. The word "pragmatic," as used for example by Americans, does not seem strong enough to do justice to the stress that Mao puts on practice as the source, goal, and truth-criterion of theoretical knowledge.

When the third dialectical phase of the cognition process, the phase of knowledge-into-practice, has been completed, is the movement of knowledge then completed? Mao's answer is: yes and no. If the knowledge has been completely applied and if the objectives foreseen have been attained—that is, if the theory-based action has changed reality in the desired way—then, in a sense, the movement of knowledge is completed. On the other hand, every practice changes the situation, alters the reality that is known. I now know how the peach tastes, but I have changed the peach by eating it. The movement of knowledge should progress and develop in keeping with the progress and development of the situation. Subjective knowledge must change as the objective situation changes or is altered by the application of knowledge. "Every process, whether in the realm of nature or of society, progresses and develops by reason of its own internal contradiction and struggle, and the movement of human knowledge should also progress and develop along with it."[36]

The key to Mao Tse-tung's ideology is the law of contradiction, the idea of the unity and the struggle of opposites. This law finds an application in Mao's conception of the relationship between practice and theory. Practice and theory form a unity of opposites; they make up a non-antagonistic contradiction. This contradiction is to be resolved by working out the theory in practice and then reformulating the theoretical knowledge so as to apply it anew.

Knowledge, then, changes with practice. And the new knowledge is related to the previous knowledge not in a linear way but by unity-in-opposition, dialectically. That is, the first theoretical knowledge is in a unity-in-opposition with its own practical application in a particular situation. There is a two-fold resolution of the contradiction; the result is a modification of the theory (in the light of how it worked) and a change in the concrete situation. The new elements in the concrete situation are in a unity-in-opposition with its earlier model. In this way, the social situation develops continuously, and theoretical knowledge develops with it, practice and theory intermingling and influencing one another's progress.

This is true, also, of the theoretical knowledge that is Mao Tse-tung thought. The teaching of Marx and Lenin was applied in practice in the Chinese communist revolution and in the building up of the new Chinese society. The resultant new theoretical knowledge is Mao's ideology. And Mao's thought, through practical application, correction, and refinement, continues to develop. That is why any effort to trace the development of Mao's thought always has to follow it through its concrete expressions and applications in the particular historical situations.[37]

Mao concludes "On Practice": "Practice knowledge, again

practice, and again knowledge. This form repeats itself in endless cycles, and with each cycle the content of practice and knowledge rises to a higher level."[38]

Mao's theory of knowledge, his philosophy of the relationship between practice and theory, is of course to be put into practice, just as the theory of knowledge itself is derived from practice. Several of Mao's writings urge research into actual social conditions before any judgments or formulations are made. He asserts, "No investigation, no right to speak."[39] The first step in any planning is to become empirically involved in the particular situation, in contact with the particular social reality in order to investigate it at first hand. "First," counsels Mao, "direct your eyes downward; do not hold your head high and gaze at the sky."[40] The second step in any investigation is to hold fact-finding meetings; the fact-finding meeting "is a better school than any university."[41] This is not only the way to investigate with a view toward planning; it is the way to learn in general. "Reading is learning, but applying is also learning and the more important kind of learning at that."[42] For Mao, all education must be in close touch with social reality; it must begin and end in practice. Learning is through experience and, then, reflection and assimilation; these are followed by testing and verifying what one has learned by applying it in the concrete.

Mao's theory of practice-knowledge and his law of contradiction are the two basic principles of his idea of organizational communications. This idea of communications within human society is the chief element in Mao's ideology of organization.

Communication and Unity

Perhaps the most important expression-in-action of any ideology is the form that the ideology takes in an organization's communications system. Since Mao Tse-tung thought is completely action-oriented, a practical ideology directed to changing reality, his teaching on communications within organized society is, together with the law of contradiction and the practice-theory-practice conception of learning, one of the three key parts of his ideology. The central concept in Mao's theory of organizational communications is that of "from the masses, to the masses," described especially clearly in his 1943 essay, "Some Questions Concerning Methods of Leadership."[43]

Government and the masses tend always to be alienated from one another; they are in a unity of opposites. The governing leaders, then, must strive for unity with the masses and remain in close contact with them. In making policy, the policy-making leaders must be in personal touch with at least some points at the most practical level of the operation they are leading; the leader should be in close contact with particular individuals and events in particular subordinate units. Only in this way will one have the concrete experience necessary for leadership. Leaders should, in this way, listen to what the masses are saying, doing, and feeling, so that the policies made by leadership will be "from the masses" as well as policies for and "to the masses."

One important method of maintaining close communications between leaders and masses is that of the leadership group. A leadership group is composed of the leaders together with some activist members of the masses. For example, a school of a hundred people should have a nucleus of leadership, a leading group of several or a dozen or more "of the most active, upright, and alert of the teachers, the other staff, and the students."[44] This method is to be applied to every organization, for example to every military unit, to every school, to every factory, and to every village and town.

Mao applies his theory of knowledge to organizational communications:

"From the masses, to the masses." This means: take the ideas of the masses (scattered and unsystematic ideas) and concentrate them (into concentrated and systematic ideas), then go to the masses and propagate and explain these ideas until the masses embrace them as their own, hold fast to them and translate them into action, and test the correctness of these ideas in such action. Then once again concentrate ideas from the masses and once again go to the masses so that the ideas are persevered in and carried through. And so on, over and over again in an endless spiral, with the ideas becoming more correct, more vital, and richer each time. Such is the Marxist theory of knowledge.[45]

When there is no active nucleus of leadership, or when this leadership group does not remain in close touch with the masses, the result is that leadership becomes bureaucratic and alienated from the masses. For Mao, then, every organization, and every unit of every organization, should be a learning system in which all levels—leadership, middle level or staff, masses—are continuously learning from one another through practice.

Mao's idea of communications, of the organization as a practice-theory-practice learning system, is not a theory of centralized leadership. It is, rather, a theory of decentralization or, more exactly, a concept of many centers, hierarchically ordered in various centralized clusters of centers, all of which are ultimately centered on the one central leadership. This system provides for maximum communication as well as for maximum responsibility and initiative at the lower, local, levels.

What gives the unity to an organizational unit or even to the Chinese nation as a whole? In Mao Tse-tung thought, what is the bond of organizational unity? Love is not ruled out, although, for Mao, in a class society there can be only class love. There can be no love transcending classes; this would be an abstract kind of love, inexistent.[46] In Mao's ideology, the emphasis is on service, on selfless devotion. Love, in other words, is understood dynamically, as in operation, as taking concrete shape in service. It is selfless service of the cause of the people that gives value to life and also to hard work, to suffering, and even to death. "The Chinese people," Mao writes, "are suffering; it is our duty to save them, and we must exert ourselves in struggle. Wherever there is struggle there is sacrifice, and death is a common occurrence. . . . When we die for the people, it is a worthy death."[47] Mao praises "devotion to others without any

thought of self" and "warm-heartedness towards all comrades
and the people."[48] "The spirit of absolute selflessness" makes a
person "useful to the people," "of value to the people."[49]

II
CHRISTIAN DOCTRINE AND MAO TSE-TUNG THOUGHT

What does Christian doctrine have to say to Mao's ideology? In what basic ways do the teachings of Christianity complement and in some way complete and fulfill Mao's teaching? The answer to this question, from a Christian point of view, depends on how the question is asked. Here, I would like to phrase the question in this way: What are the areas or elements in Mao's thought that open up to Christian teaching in such a way that those areas or elements can be seen to be incomplete, can be understood as open-ended, as questions for which Christianity is able to indicate answers or at least lines of completion? My approach, then, is that of "apologetics" in the classic and traditional sense. The method is one of correlation, of correlating certain foundational problems that appear in Mao Tsetung thought with appropriate Christian doctrines that indicate, in one way or another, solutions to those problems. The result will be a brief sketch of some points for an *apologia* for Christianity in confrontation with Mao's ideology. The idea is, at a theoretical level, to dialogue with contemporary Chinese ideology so as to "go in their door" and "come out" in the domain of Christian teaching. My purpose, therefore, is not to refute Mao's teachings. Instead, I have a maximally positive aim: to see where Mao Tse-tung thought and Christian doctrine meet and might fit together. This is, admittedly, a somewhat naive and perhaps overly intellectualist approach. But dialogue has to begin somewhere. And Christian dialogue with non-Christian or even anti-Christian cultures and ideologies begins with looking for those things in the culture or in the ideology which are, in Tertullian's expression, "naturally Christian." These elements are to be identified, appealed to, worked with, corrected, and built upon. There appear to be at least three such elements in

Mao's ideology: his idea of universal struggle, including the idea of permanent revolution; his notion of ideology or basic principles of doing and his concept of unity.

Struggle and Christian Hope

Mao Tse-tung thought is, to use a Christian term, eschatological, as is any belief system that sees and gives weight to the fact that things in the present are not as they should be, but they can get better. Every revolutionary ideology is eschatological. Ideologies have force not because they coincide with reality, but because they point the way to a better future.[50] Mao's eschatology, however, is incomplete. Human progress, whether of the individual person or of humanity itself, has—in Mao's thought —no ultimate goal. Not only does each person die and simply go out of existence, but the human race itself will either die or change into something else to disappear forever. That is to say, in Mao's ideology there is no solution to the problem of death. "Well," Sancho Panza tells Don Quixote, "there's a remedy for everything except death, under whose yoke we all have to come, whether we like it or not, when life's finished."[51]

The traditional Christian answer to the problem of death is personal and collective immortality. It is, in particular, the question of collective immortality that is the opening of Mao Tse-tung thought to Christian teaching. The question is: "After the permanent revolution, then what?" The question and its answer are important. Mao's ideology is perhaps the clearest formulation of the widespread contemporary consciousness that people are moving rapidly into a future for which they are becoming more and more aware that they are responsible. In those parts of the world where human progress is most rapid, the future-directedness of humanity is most clearly becoming an essential element of human consciousness, of the general world view of people.

The contemporary primacy of the future, particularly in the case of Mao's ideology as one expression of humankind's current future-orientation, gives rise to the problem of hope.

Hope is the quality of the human spirit that looks to the future and that gives the momentum to take the necessary steps into that future. Hope becomes increasingly a problem and a search for faith in some ground or anchor for hope as the future-directedness of a culture or an ideology becomes deeper and more important in the collective awareness of a society. Inevitably, Mao Tse-tung thought as the ideology of millions of Chinese is a question that, increasingly, will need some kind of answer; it is an optimistic ideology that looks to the future, to progress, to further human and social development and that will necessarily, and more and more, find itself asking where the whole human enterprise—and especially the building of the new China—is going. The question is not simply about the future but about the ultimate future.

The ultimate future of humanity as foreseen by Mao is its extinction, either by the death of the human race or by its transformation into something else. The death of the species: this prospect is surely due to provoke a collective anxiety as the new China builds itself toward the future. If beyond progress there is only the dead end of the mass grave, then the sickness of the dead end is going to set in and grow, unless there is found a basis for hope in an ultimate future.

The conditions for such a hope are two: that it be in a person, for people can hope only in persons, not ultimately in ideologies and plans; and that there be the assurance of an ultimately successful outcome for the enterprise of human progress. The Christian teaching of a world to come, of an ultimate collective future centered on Jesus Christ risen, fulfills those conditions. Jesus risen is precisely that person whose hands hold the ultimate future of each person and of all humanity. He is the ground of Christian hope, the anchor. The place where Christian hope stands is on personal and collective faith in the risen Jesus. He is the answer not only to the death of the individual but, as the personal Center of the world to come, to the death of human society in this world.

It is above all the Second Vatican Council that has expressed this hope doctrinally. Vatican II, especially in the Introduction to *Gaudium et spes,* the Pastoral Constitution on the

Church in the Modern World, understands the risen Christ as the future focal point of humanity's progress and as the goal of history. He is, moreover, the passage to the life to come, a life which has a real continuity with human history, and in which people will find transformed and purified all of what is best in what has been built in the present life, including interpersonal relationships in society.[52]

The continuous struggle for progress and development, the struggle at the heart of current Chinese communist ideology, is a question looking for an ultimate answer; Mao's conception of permanent revolution is one that, by its very nature and structure, asks for an ultimate justification, for an ultimate meaning. This meaning can be found in the Christian doctrine that the struggle of people on earth is or can be a participation in the struggle, in the passion, of Jesus. Just as Jesus' struggle and death ended in resurrection, so can the struggle and death of each person and of humanity collectively. The human struggle finds its ultimate meaning in the cross of Jesus and its ultimate justification in the life to come, toward which the cross is pointed.

There is, then, an internal contradiction in Mao Tse-tung thought between its stress on the struggle for the development of people and of society, its positive and optimistic orientation toward the human future, and—on the other hand—its absence of an ultimate goal to give ultimate meaning to the struggle and to be a solid basis for human hope. This is one of the contradictions interior to Mao's ideology. It is an opening of that ideology to a resolution of the contradiction through hope in the risen Christ; it is a need for and an opening out to Christian hope.

Human Existence and Faith

Mao Tse-tung's ideology is too all-encompassing and too flexible to be considered a system of thought. It is not really a philosophy in the usual sense. It is, really, a way of understanding and of working with reality. It is a practical vision containing general guidelines for action, together with a certain faith in people and in the possibilities of human progress. An action-oriented world view and a faith: these are the elements of a religion.

Teilhard de Chardin, discussing the emergence of the communist myth, writes that "it is no longer a matter of mere heresies within Christianity, but of Christianity's being confronted by what seems to be an entirely new religion."[53] What is more, the "religion" of the new China is a contemporary one, within the framework of a generally future-oriented and contemporary world view. And it is an eschatological "religion," not analogous to the eastern religions that deny the polar tension between the present and the future and that search for the tranquillity of unity through the suppression of the multiple, of pain, and of struggle. Mao's ideology is more along the lines of the two major eschatological religions, Islam and Christianity; and of the two, it is closer to Christianity. It would, of course, be pushing the matter too far to say that Mao Tse-tung thought is a truncated Christianity. But in its origins—beyond Marx and Lenin in the Christianity-rooted dialectical idealism of Hegel— as well as in its present form, it looks somewhat like the Christian religion without faith in Jesus Christ. The absence of faith in the person of Jesus implies, obviously, a radical difference between the two religions. And it is, above all, faith in Jesus that is what Christianity has to say to Mao Tse-tung thought.

In what way does Christian faith add anything essential to Mao's ideology? From a Christian point of view, taking faith in Christ as an a priori, the answer is evident. But on Mao's own terms, "going in his door," is there some fundamental lack in his thought that takes the form of a question to which Christian faith is the answer? Is there, in Mao's ideology, an opening that points to faith in Jesus, an internal contradiction of which the resolution is the faith that Christians have in Jesus Christ? Apparently, yes.

Mao's ideology is, like Christianity, not a philosophy but a way of life; it is the way that Mao calls people to live their daily lives. People are persons, and as persons they are knowing and loving subjects, able to know more and more, indefinitely, and so to love increasingly. The individual, as person, as knowing and loving subject, has an opening inside to something beyond, to something that transcends the person, to the transcendent. And because each one is person, the individual opens out to the knowledge and love of a Transcendent Personal Being, to personal relationship with God. From a human point of view, one's very existence as personal calls for a faith relationship with God.

This is the relationship to which God, present in Jesus, calls all. Jesus, in the gospels and through his Church, calls people to believe in him, to accept him and to respond to him by adhering to him, and so—through him—to be in relationship with God. And this is Christian faith; not simply an intellectual assent to certain truths, but beyond that an interpersonal relationship with God present in his saving power in Jesus. All divine revelation is contained in Jesus Christ risen, and a positive personal relationship with him implies the acceptance of the religion centered on him. This, faith in Jesus, is the heart of Christianity.

When such a faith is missing, when one lacks a positive personal relationship with the Transcendent Personal, then that person is equivalently denying an opening to that Transcendent Personal Being. In so doing, there is a denial of one's existence as a knowing and loving subject, as a person. Human dignity and human freedom are, existentially, rooted in the opening out to God that everyone has at the core of existence. When human openness to God is denied, suppressed, or ignored, the ground is cut out from under personal dignity and freedom.

There is no question but that Mao Tse-tung thought contains a great compassion for humanity, especially for the oppressed, the suffering, the radically poor. And, further, its purpose is human development, of the person and of society—for the two cannot be separated. What is missing is the necessary basis for Mao's compassion and for his purpose to make more real, in the concrete, human dignity and human freedom. Without such a basis, the purpose is undermined from the beginning. Ideology is not enough; it is, by itself, always lacking a center; that center is the center of people themselves, the opening out to

God that is the ground of one's dignity and freedom and possibilities as a person.

An ideology that tries to take humankind seriously as subject, as person, will always fail in practice unless it is built around one of the very things that Mao's ideology rejects, personal faith in a personal God who takes everyone seriously as a personal subject. It will inevitably end by treating people not as subjects but as objects. And this is the problem with Mao Tse-tung thought. But it is a problem, an internal contradiction, that is looking for a solution, for a resolution. It is a question for which Christianity has, at its heart, the answer.

Unity and Christian Love

Love, at least class love in selfless devotion to the people, is important in Mao's thought. So is unity, although Mao stresses communication rather than love or service as the basis of unity. That is, his interest is more in how to facilitate unity through the practice of listening and learning rather than in selfless service as the bond of unity. The reason for this seems to lie at least partially in Mao's conception of unity; unity is always a unity of opposites and so in some way a "contradiction." The unity of "the people" or of a class is a non-antagonistic unity of opposition. The advantage of seeing unity in terms of non-antagonistic contradictions is that the idea of complementarity is brought out. As a matter of fact, Mao's non-antagonistic contradiction does seem to be a unity of complementaries rather than a unity of opposites; this is in continuity with the traditional Ying-Yang type of Chinese thinking. What Mao does not underline is love as the bond of unity.

Certainly the Christian idea of unity as community of love has something to say on this point to Mao Tse-tung thought. Even more, Mao's avoidance of any emphasis on love as the bond that unites people betrays a central lacuna in the Maoist concept of unity, an absence that Christian teaching on love and unity is able to fill. What Mao misses is the need for some personal and synthesizing Center of love.

In Christian teaching, the primacy is given to love, and above all to the love with which God loves people first. And, although the Christian obligation is summed up in the duty to love God and to love one another, the force to fulfill this law comes from God himself who, through Jesus, pours the Spirit of love into human hearts. It is the Spirit of Jesus that enables people to fulfill the commandment to love one another. It is the human condition to have the tendency to seek one's own welfare even at the expense of others, to get for oneself riches and honors and security. Humankind's narcissism, even in the most optimistic reading of human potential, is ingrained in the structure of the individual's this-world existence. The call to selfless service can be, by and large, answered honestly only by a force in people that, while its own, is God's gift to it. This force is centralized in and comes from the risen Jesus.

There is, moreover, a human need for a Personal Center of love to synthesize all a person's commitments. The positive relationships in anyone's life, the relationships of love in diverse forms—family, social unit, patriotism, devotion to a cause—need some kind of integrating factor to unify them, to bring them together so that the forces of love are not scattered. Because love is essentially a personal activity, this integrating factor must be a Personal Center capable of sustaining and organizing all of a person's love relationships. It must therefore be a Center that transcends all simply human loves so as to unite them into one, and a Center that transcends all people so as to unite them into one. It must also be human even though it transcends the human. For Christianity, this transcendent Personal Center of love is Jesus Christ risen. Christian unity is community in and centered on the risen Jesus.

The nature and meaning of love are seen in the cross. There is, in this world, no love without suffering, because love means going out of oneself toward others in selfless devotion and service. But the cross derives its meaning and its motive force from the resurrection of Jesus in which all people can share just as they share in his cross.

The internal contradiction in Mao's ideas about unity and service is this: the call to unity, while aided by communication, can only be fulfilled by loving; selfless devotion is love's activity and can be accomplished only in love; but love, to truly exist and to persevere, needs a transcendent Center that is personal and loving. This Center is missing in Mao's ideology. The lack of such a Center is the opening of Mao Tse-tung thought to Christian teaching on love.

To sum up, from a brief analysis of Mao's thought, three fundamental contradictions (using the word "contradiction" in the Maoist sense) appear. A first contradiction exists between the permanent call to revolutionary struggle and the lack of an ultimate personal goal to give hope and meaning to the struggle. A second contradiction comes into sight when a solid foundation for human dignity and freedom is looked for and found missing. The third contradiction is between Mao's call to service in unity and the fact of the absence of a force-giving and organizing Center of love. All three of these internal contradictions look to a resolution. The Christian resolution takes the forms of Christian hope, Christian faith, and Christian love, all centered on the risen Jesus.

III
MAO TSE-TUNG THOUGHT AND CHRISTIAN THEOLOGY

Dialogue is a two-way street. If Christian teaching has something to say to Mao's ideology, how can Christian theology profit from Mao's teachings? Mao Tse-tung thought is what Vatican II calls a sign of the times. In Mao's thought is gathered together much of what is best in contemporary humankind's aspirations; Mao's ideology has something to say to Christian theology.

Theology has as its task to bring God's Word to expression so that it can be addressed to people. Theology is at the service of the proclamation of God's Word. In order that the Word may be addressed to the people it must be formulated in the thought categories of the times. Insofar as Mao Tse-tung thought is a sign of the times, a complexus of the vision and purpose of the new China and at the same time a way of approaching reality that appeals to many outside communist China, it can be useful to Christian theology. Its usefulness is not in that it adds in some way to the content of what Christians hold, but in that it can provide new ways of seeing and understanding Christian truth so as to apply that truth in Christian life.

Here, I would like to suggest three areas in which Maoist thought might help Christian theology in bringing to expression, in formulating, God's Word to people in Jesus. These areas are: the meaning of the cross, the relationship between theology and Christian life, and the theology of the church as a learning community.

Struggle and the Cross

The new China's struggle for human progress has a positive significance for Christianity. St. Augustine's description and evaluation of the "earthly city" can be applied to communist China today.

> The earthly city, which shall not be everlasting . . . has its good in this world and rejoices in it with such joy as such things can afford. But as this is not a good which can discharge its devotees of all distresses, this city is often divided against itself by litigations, wars, quarrels. . . . But the things that the earthly city desires cannot justly said to be evil, for this kind of good is, at its own level, better than all other human good. These things, then, are good things, and without doubt God's gifts.[54]

Pierre Teilhard de Chardin, the Jesuit scientist, has gone even further in saying that he

> absolutely refuses to admit that atheism is an organic part of Marxism: Marxism does not deny the *whole God,* but only the God of the Above, in the *measure that* this God seems incompatible with the God of the Forward. From

this, there is a perspective of mutual understanding between the Christian and the Marxist *in the perspective* of a
world in a state of total evolution (but only in such a perspective).[55]

These two quotations should be read in the context of the teaching of Vatican II's Pastoral Constitution on the Church in the
Modern World, *Gaudium et spes*. In this, perhaps the most important of the Council documents, the world view is evolu-
tionary, that of a world in genesis, in development. In *Gaudium
et spes*, human progress is viewed as ambiguous because of the
variable that is human freedom; nonetheless, humanity's
progress in this world is in continuity with the world to come
and is of vital importance to the kingdom of God.[56] At the same
time, the conception of history is Christocentric: "Jesus Christ
is the goal of human history, the focal point of the longings of
history and civilization, the center of the human race, the joy of
every heart and the answer to all its yearnings."[57] Therefore,
"men are not deterred by the Christian message from building
up the world, or impelled to neglect the welfare of their fellows,
but rather they are more stringently bound to do these very
things."[58]

Before the Second Vatican Council, Christian theology,
and especially Roman Catholic theology, tended to over-
emphasize what might be called the upward, vertical component
of Christianity at the expense of the forward and horizontal component. It stressed the other-worldly dimensions of Christian
faith much more than the this-world dimensions that call the
Christian to social responsibility. Since the Council this situation
has been somewhat remedied, particularly with the theologies
of secularity, of hope, and of liberation. But an important
problem remains: the theological *integration* of the vertical
and the horizontal, of the upward and the forward.

It seems to me that theology can find in Mao's ideology elements for a theology of the Incarnation and of the cross that
can accomplish this integration, that can aid theology to formu-
late faith so that humanity's struggle for human development,
both of the person and of society, can be seen as a participation
in the life and death of Jesus and as the avenue toward the goal

of that struggle, the reconciliation of all things in the risen Jesus. I will indicate briefly a few points for reflection on how this might be done.

The Incarnation can be understood as a non-antagonistic (complementary) contradiction, as a unity of opposites in which those opposites, the divinity and the humanity of Jesus, are unified in a productive union. This approach to the Incarnation is in harmony with that of the early councils of the Church, especially the Councils of Ephesus and Chalcedon, and with the writings of the great medieval scholastic theologians. In Jesus, God joins himself to humankind and through it to the world. In the Incarnation, God and the world become mutual, enter into a mutuality that is the fulfillment of the Old Testament covenant.

In his public life and in his passion and death, Jesus is in an antagonistic contradiction with the powers of darkness, with the forces of sin and death and of all that oppresses people. The public ministry of Jesus can be seen as including a non-antagonistic contradiction between Jesus and the religion of Israel. Jesus is one side of a unity of opposites; the other side is the traditional Jewish religion that he came to fulfill. This complementary unity of opposites gives rise, as Jesus continues his ministry, to an antagonistic contradiction with the leaders of the Jewish religion. The powers of darkness, working through the antagonistic unity-in-opposition between Jesus and the Jewish leadership, bring to a culmination the fundamental antagonistic contradiction, that between Jesus and the forces of sin and death. This culmination is the crucifixion of Jesus.

In the dialectic categories of Engels, the death of Jesus could be considered as the "negation of the negation." Jesus' death negates the negative powers of darkness including those negativities that are death and sin. Jesus does this by submitting to the summation of all evils, death; but his submission—the "hour" of the forces of evil—is in reality the negation of those very forces. This understanding of the redemptive act of the cross corresponds to the usual conception of Jesus' death as an expiation, reparation, and satisfaction for sin, and it fits with Luther's theology of the crucifixion of Jesus as vicarious suffering for sinful humanity.

An understanding of the cross in Maoist categories, howev-

er, goes further. In Mao Tse-tung thought, the law of the negation of the negation does not exist; every negation is, at the
same time, an affirmation. The negation of people's possibilities
by evil and finally by death is, simultaneously, the affirmation
of the forces of evil. And Jesus' negation of the forces of evil is
also, and more importantly, the affirmation of humanity and of
human possibilities, especially the liberation from evil and salvation to God. Jesus' conquest of death by dying on the cross is
the affirmation of life for everyone; his victory over sin is the affirmation of God's gracious and powerful love that saves people. The cross of Jesus, because it is ordered to Jesus' resurrection and to humankind's salvation, is not only a negation; it is
as much or more an affirmation.

The antagonistic contradiction between Jesus and the
powers of darkness is a struggle for development, for the
progress of people toward God. And it is a revolutionary struggle, because Jesus—by his death—creates a new order for humanity, the order of grace and of life in the Spirit. The cross of
Jesus, then, is the reality and the symbol of the human struggle
for more life, for development, for liberation from all that oppresses; it is the symbol of the struggle in this life through the
world and in society toward God, toward the future that God
has destined in Jesus for those whom he loves.

The results of Jesus' saving death on the cross are being
worked out in history. The victory of the cross of Jesus is, in
principle, complete. But that victory has not yet been completed
as to its application to human history. All things are recapitu-
lated and reconciled in Jesus through his death on the cross, but
that recapitulation and that reconciliation will not be finally accomplished in the concrete conditions of history until history is
finished and the world to come begins. Humanity, in history,
lives in the existential structure of the cross of Jesus, a cross
that is ordered to resurrection.

The Christian has been baptized into the structure of the
death of Jesus, and so the struggle of the Christian, and of all
people insofar as they live somehow in Christ, is a participation
in Jesus' cross. Jesus' command to his followers, that they take
up their crosses and follow him, can be understood as a com-

mand to share with him the struggle against all that oppresses humanity, the struggle for the affirmation of persons and for their personal and societal development and progress. The cross in the life of the Christian is the symbol and the reality of the effort through hard work and suffering and finally death to build a fuller life, a more human society, and a better future in the direction of the ultimate future that will end the struggle and bring to completion the victory of the cross.

Christian love is a love that takes the shape of selfless service of others, of a going out of oneself to others. In this going out of oneself in service, the Christian finds the cross. This is the connection between the cross and the struggle for the liberation of humanity from oppression. In this way, the cross—as the symbol of the struggle to liberate people to a more human life—has a strong social dimension. The Christian is called to move into the future toward the risen Jesus who is the goal of history; this movement into the future takes the form of a selfless service of others, a service in the shape of the cross.[59]

Life and Theology

Theology is faith seeking to understand itself. All Christians, therefore, are to some extent theologians, since all are called to bring into always greater awareness and into clearer personal formulation the faith that God calls them to live out in their daily lives. Mao's thought, in its conception of the relationship between practice and theory, has a contribution to make to Christian theology regarding the relationship between life and the understanding and formulation of faith.

Christian faith is, first of all, relational; it is an interpersonal relationship with God present in Jesus Christ, a relationship to be lived out. Christian faith is a faith-to-be-done, to be practiced in the concrete circumstances of life. "The truth of the gospel," writes Gustavo Gutiérrez, "is something to be *done*. In the Bible, truth lies between promise and achievement and not in the approximation between concept and reality."[60] Since the truth of Christian religion is ordered to practice, it is necessarily ordered to the future. This is the main reason why metaphysical speculation no longer is, nor can be, central to the theological enterprise. Not only does the contemporary world think and act in terms of the future, with a certain future-directedness, but the very truth of Christianity itself is future-oriented. Metaphysics studies what-is, not what-is-not; it cannot handle what-is-not-yet: the future. Metaphysics is still and may always be important in theology; it will never again be a central preoccupation.

Maoist ideology reminds Christians that a "practice-theory-practice" learning system is just as Christian as it is Maoist. The formulation of Christian truth, the bringing to expression of faith, should begin with Christian life and practice. The task of theology is to reflect on lived Christian experience. This is nothing new; *praxis ecclesiae,* the practice of the Christian community, has always been—at least sporadically or theoretically—the principal source for theological reflection. "Practice-theory-practice," however, goes further than that. It says that theology must not be only rooted in practice, but that it must be in continuous contact with practice. Armchair or ivory-tower theology is not truly Christian.

Perhaps even more importantly for Christian theology, Mao's thought on practice and theory reminds Christians that theology should be *ordered to* practice, that the formulation of faith must have as its aim the fuller practice of Christian truth. Theology must begin with Christian life, remain in touch with life, and aim at Christian living. This is where the two greatest medieval theologians, Thomas Aquinas and John Duns Scotus, can be brought together regarding theology's purpose. For Thomas, theology strives for truth; for Scotus, theology aims at practice. But it comes to the same thing when Christian truth is understood as truth-to-be-practiced.

Traditionally, the best theology has reflected on experience in the light of Jesus Christ and, in that light, explained experience. There is nothing wrong with that, but much more seems to be needed. Primarily, Christianity needs theology that will describe the action needed to transform the world in Christ. What Christianity needs is not so much theology that searches the antecedent reasons for faith, that seeks the conditions of possibili-

ty of the Christian mysteries so that they may be better understood. The primary need is for a theology of consequences, for
theology that tells how to live and how to act, for an action-
oriented theology. The models for this kind of theology are not
Thomas Aquinas, nor Scotus, nor most contemporary theologians. The models are Ignatius Loyola, Teresa of Avila, John of
the Cross, George Fox, and above all Saint Paul.

The need, then, is for theology that presents a vision that is
ordered to action. But would this not result in ideology rather
than theology? No. The result would be theology with strong
ideological elements, yes. But Christianity is centered on the
Person of Jesus Christ; this is why it is not an ideology. Theology, too, should always center itself in one way or another on
Jesus, and so can and should remain essentially non-ideological,
although containing ideological elements, principles of concrete
action.

Communications and Community

The first four centuries of the church's history saw the
evolution and precision of the theological formulation of the
doctrines of the Trinity and the Incarnation; there is still much
theology to be done today in these areas, but Christian thought
laid the theological foundations of these mysteries before Saint
Augustine. In the time of Augustine theological interest centered on the doctrine of divine grace and human need for that
grace. Every Christian age has had a theological focus. Today
the key area of theological concern is the theology of the
church. The current controversies on infallibility, on church authority, on the mission of the church, and on church structures
manifest the theological ferment regarding the Christian community.

What appears to be missing in contemporary theological
reflection on the church is a theology of communications. The
theology of the church needs a theology of communications as a
basis for considering and evaluating church organization from a
communications point of view, for looking at the church as a
learning system. Mao Tse-tung thought, with its principle of

"from the masses, to the masses," can stimulate Christian reflection on the church as a learning system.

It might be argued that the Roman Catholic understanding
of church authority precludes, at least for Catholic theology,
any worthwhile thinking about the church as a "from the
masses, to the masses" system of learning. The church teaches,
one might say; it learns from God, not from "the masses." And
the church's authority does not come from the people; it comes
from God. Authority comes from the top down, and so, too,
teaching is from the top down; to oversimplify somewhat, the
church leaders teach and the people learn. However, where authority comes from and how it is exercised in practice are not
the same thing. What Mao says about Chinese communist leadership and its relationship with the people would seem to be
applicable also to Christian leadership and its relationship with
the people of God. There is no logical contradiction between
church authority and a "from the people, to the people" learning system; there is however a non-antagonistic contradiction in
the Maoist sense. Church authority stands in a complementary
unity of opposites with the Christian faithful. The unity must be
reinforced through love, but communication forms the basis of
love and so of unity.

Parish boards, priests' senates, national and regional conferences of bishops, bishops' synods, and grass roots movements
like the charismatic and cursillo movements are all structural
beginnings for better communication from and to the people.
These beginnings need a theology of the church as learning system, a theology that starts in the actual practice of communication and, resting in contact with that practice, reflects on it
and orders its reflections to better communication in all direc-
tions. Such a theology could use modern sociology and theories
of groups and of communications, but it ought to ground itself
in present concrete situations.

When Mao Tse-tung's ideas of "practice-theory-practice"
and of "from the masses, to the masses" are taken together, as
they exist in Mao's thought, then there arise enormous implications not only for church government but also for the formation
of priests and other religious professionals and, also, for catechetics and religious education. Formation programs for reli-

gious congregations and for the priesthood and related minis-
tries are already moving rapidly in a more practical direction
through the implementation of internships, practical experiences, and more open discussion and sharing at the levels where
practice and theory come together. These efforts need an overall
framework for reflection, principles to operate from, that will
help formation periods to take place in specialized learning systems that begin in practice and that through reflection move to
improved practice.

In the general field of religious education and catechetics,
too, Mao's concept of learning through practice and of keeping
contacts between leadership and lower levels speaks to the present situation. Can personal relationship with God be communicated without the practical learning of prayer, both individual
and group? Can Christian community be taught apart from its
continuous practice? And can service be inculcated without
practice on the part of those who learn to serve? In learning the
processes of prayer, community, and service, learning begins
and—through reflection—ends in the practice of those processes. And, in all of this, the need exists for continuous contact
between learners and various levels of church leadership.

Christians can and must learn from the signs of the times.
One important such "sign" of our times, Mao Tse-tung
thought, stands out. Christians, I suggest, are called to read that
sign not just or even primarily with a view to the eventual
evangelization of the new China or of the many developing
countries influenced by Chinese communist ideology. More importantly, Mao's ideology can speak to the Christian need for
personal development, for the evolution of the total Christian
community, and for more productive Christian action and
thought.

NOTES

1. J. Ching, "The Christian Way and Chinese Wall," *America*,
Nov. 9, 1974, p. 278.
2. "Speech at the Supreme State Conference," *Chairman Mao
Talks to the People*, ed. S. Schram (Pantheon: New York, 1974) p. 94.

3. See J.B. Starr, *Ideology and Culture* (Harper and Row: New York, 1973) pp. 24-29; see also F. Schurmann, *Ideology and Organization in Communist China* (University of California: Berkeley, 1966) pp. 19-23.

4. "On the Ten Great Relationships," *Chairman Mao Talks to the People*, pp. 61-83.

5. *Selected Readings from the Works of Mao Tse-tung* (Foreign Languages Press: Peking, 1967) pp. 70-108, and pp. 350-387.

6. "On Contradiction," *Selected Readings*, p. 70.

7. *Ibid.*, p. 72.

8. See D. Munro, "The Malleability of Man in Chinese Marxism," *The China Quarterly*, no. 48 (1971) pp. 609-640.

9. See S. Schram, "Mao Tse-tung and the Theory of the Permanent Revolution," *The China Quarterly*, no. 46 (1971) pp. 221-244.

10. "On Contradiction," p. 74.

11. "On the Correct Handling of Contradictions among the People," Selected Readings, op. cit., p. 358.

12. "On Contradiction," p. 70.

13. *Ibid.*, p. 76.

14. See J.B. Starr, *Ideology and Culture*, pp. 26-27.

15. "Talk on Questions of Philosophy," *Chairman Mao Talks to the People*, p. 226.

16. *Ibid.*

17. "On Contradiction," p. 101.

18. *Ibid.*, p. 96.

19. "Talks at Chengtu," *Chairman Mao Talks to the People*, p. 109.

20. "Tingchow to Changsha," *The Poems of Mao Tse-tung*, tr. W. Barnstone (Harper and Row: New York, 1972) p. 49.

21. "On Contradiction," p. 103. The Cultural Revolution (1965-1969) is a recent example of an intra-party antagonistic contradiction.

22. Mao's "Analysis of the Classes in Chinese Society," 1926, *Selected Readings, op. cit.*, pp. 11-19, gives a detailed sociological categorization of classes; this conception evolved eventually into a purely ideological classification. See also, "On Democratic Centralism," 1962, *Chairman Mao Talks to the People*, pp. 169-170.

23. "Sixty Work Methods (Draft): The General Office of the Central Committee of the Communist Party of China" (February, 1958), quoted in F. Wakeman, *History and Will* (University of California: Berkeley, 1973) p. 236.

24. "On the Correct Handling of Contradictions Among the People," p. 358.

25. *Selected Readings*, pp. 54-69. Just as typically, western commentators on Mao's political theory invariably speak of "theory and practice," putting "theory" first.

26. *Ibid.*, pp. 58-59.

27. *Ibid.*, p. 59.

28. *Ibid.*, p. 60.
29. *Selected Readings*, p. 405.
30. "On Practice," p. 61.
31. *Ibid.*, p. 63.
32. *Ibid.*
33. *Ibid.*
34. *Ibid.*, p. 64. In a later essay (1963), "Where Do Correct Ideas Come From?", Mao writes that generally speaking ideas "that succeed are correct; those that fail are incorrect." (*Selected Readings*, p. 405.)
35. Starr, *op. cit.*, pp. 29-30.
36. "On Practice," p. 65.
37. See J. Ch'en, "The Development and Logic of Mao Tse-tung's Thought." *Ideology and Politics in Contemporary China*, ed. C. Johnson (University of Washington: Seattle, 1973) pp. 78-114.
38. "On Practice," p. 67.
39. "Preface to Rural Surveys," *Selected Readings*, p. 160; "Oppose Book Worship," *ibid.*, pp. 33-34.
40. "Preface to Rural Surveys," p. 158.
41. *Ibid.*, p. 159.
42. "The Important Thing is to be Good at Learning," *Selected Readings*, p. 51; the essay concerns warfare; Mao writes that "our chief method is to learn warfare through warfare" (*ibid.*, p. 51).
43. *Selected Readings*, pp. 234-239.
44. *Ibid.*, p. 236.
45. *Ibid.*
46. "Talks at the Yenan Forum on Literature and Art," *Selected Readings*, p. 209.
47. "Serve the People," *ibid.*, p. 253.
48. "In Memory of Norman Bethune," *ibid.*, p. 146.
49. *Ibid.*, p. 147.
50. F. Wakeman, Jr., points out that a "restless sense of purpose motivates all revolutionary movements; and unless we appreciate its vigor, we will never truly understand the dynamism of Chinese ideology" ("The Use and Abuse of Ideology in the Study of Contemporary China," *The China Quarterly*, no. 61, 1975) p. 152.
51. Miguel de Cervantes, *Don Quixote*, Part II, chapter 10.
52. Part 1, chapters 3 and 4.
53. "The Awaited Word," *Toward the Future*, tr. R. Hague (Harcourt Brace Jovanovich: New York, 1975) p. 95.
54. *The City of God*, Book 15, chapter 4.
55. Unpublished letter of May 21, 1952, to Francois Richaud. For other reflections by Teilhard de Chardin on Marxism and on the communist movement, see the following essays in *The Future of Man*, tr. N. Denny (Harper and Row: New York, 1964): "Some Reflections on the Rights of Man," pp. 193-195; "Faith in Man," pp. 185-192. on the convergence of Marxism and Christianity; "The Heart of the Matter,"

pp. 260-269. See also: "The Salvation of Mankind," *Science and Christ,* tr. R. Hague (Harper and Row: New York, 1969) pp. 128-150; and the brief comments in "The Planetisation of Mankind," *The Future of Man, op. cit.,* p. 139, and in "The Awaited Word," *Toward the Future,* tr. R. Hague (Harcourt Brace Jovanovich: New York, 1975) p. 95. A good commentary on Teilhard's views on Marxism is: C. Cuénot, "Teilhard et le marxisme," *Europe,* nos. 431-2 (March-April, 1965) pp. 164-185.

56. Part I, chapter. 3.

57. Part I, chapter 4.

58. Part I, chapter 3.

59. See R. Whitehead, "Love and Animosity in the Ethic of Mao," *Båstad,* pp. 71-85. Whitehead calls for a theology of struggle and asks how it can be related to the self-emptying of the cross. This part of the present study takes its inspiration partly from Whitehead's article.

60. G. Gutiérrez, "Theology and the Chinese Experience," *Louvain,* p. 104.

The New China and God's Plan for Salvation

DOMENICO GRASSO, S.J.

The New China represents a problem for the Church: I do not think anyone can doubt that. Commissioned by Christ to preach the Gospel to every creature (Mark 16:16), the Church today finds itself unable to send its missionaries into a country whose citizens number one fourth of the world's population, and which, in little more than twenty-five years, has gained an international prestige that it would be a serious mistake to underestimate. The New China represents a point of reference and a model for the third-world countries that are seeking a way out of their state of under-development without losing their political, economic, and cultural independence. The New China can be an incalculable hindrance or help to the mission of the Church: a hindrance if, satisfied with its own achievements, it insists that it has no need of religion—and still less of Christianity—in order to develop its own form of society that others will eagerly imitate; but a help if, entering into dialog with Christianity, it comes to see that the Christian message has something to offer that China lacks: indeed, something that it is seeking, without realizing it.

In our opinion it is precisely on the level of theology that dialog is needed between the New China and the rest of the world. In terms of material benefits, China already has—or will soon be able to provide for itself—all that the western nations could offer it. Indeed, judging by the necessarily limited information at our disposal, China seems to be achieving this material progress while at the same time avoiding the defects—not to use a stronger term—into which western culture has fallen. We

81

are told that in China one does not find the violence, the alcoholism, the crime, the social inequities, the unbridled materialism, that are so evident in western civilization. China has created, or at least is on the way to creating, a "consumer culture," without the drawbacks that have accompanied such a culture in its western form. It is impossible for us to evaluate this success in its exact proportions, but if what we are told is true, it could provide a model and a stimulus, not only to developing countries, but to developed ones as well.

Moreover, and this is the factor of greatest interest to us, the scientific and social achievements of the New China have been realized following the thought of Mao Tse-tung: a thought that is fundamentally materialistic, and that makes of class-struggle, not only the originating but also the permanent principle of social development. According to Mao, it is not enough to have achieved a classless society; even after this goal is achieved, class-struggle must continue, in order to crush every tendency toward "revisionism," or such a revival of capitalism as the Chinese claim has taken place in Russia.

In this doctrine we have an interpretation of the social process that we do not find in classical Marxism: this is Mao's answer to those who see in Communism a model of development which is doomed to fall back into the very system against which it struggled, and whose defects it so effectively revealed.

If, therefore, a dialog between the West and the New China is going to be meaningful, it will have to find other ground than the socio-economic, in which area Mao has realized his most spectacular successes. This ground of dialog cannot be other than the religious. Mao has seen in the traditional religions of his country nothing but an obstacle to social progress, and he has sought to destroy their hold on the people by emptying them of their meaning. Buddhism, Taoism and Confucianism all claimed to offer to humanity the values necessary for a truly human life. Mao has shown that his vision of history, and the model of development which he has worked out, offer something much more valuable. The struggle against Confucianism is typical. Confucius aimed at the formation of the "wise man": that is, of the cultivated person, capable of providing leadership for the rest of society. Mao rejects this idea, because for him, what counts are the masses, which find in themselves, without having to receive it from anyone, the principles and the strength to provide their own leadership in the creation of a new society.

If there is one religion with which Mao could enter into dialog, it is Christianity: the universal religion, which speaks about what is most personal to human beings, about their most basic problems. What is the meaning of life, of history? This is the true problem of people, the one that must inspire a vision of the world, if this vision is not going to be partial and provisory, but such as can explain history both in its ongoing process and in its beginning and end. The problem which the Maoist sooner or later must confront is precisely the one to which Christianity can give the answer. Why should one sacrifice oneself for another? Maoism demands of its followers a perpetual asceticism, a spirit of total self-sacrifice, a dedication to service of others that no obstacle is allowed to bring to a halt. But inevitably the question will present itself: Why all this sacrifice? Who is the "other" for whom I am asked to sacrifice myself? What meaning can a life lived for others have, if everything is going to end in death? Is it worthwhile to sacrifice myself for someone who is eventually going to end in the same nothingness to which I, myself, am doomed?

Someday the Maoist is going to have to face these questions. When the enthusiasm of the pioneering days has passed, the Maoist will enter into a phase of reflection in which all that has been accomplished will be subjected to judgment and evaluation. This is what has taken place in western society. After creating a style of life in which it seemed that humanity could want for nothing more, at last it had to ask itself what the meaning of all this could be. This questioning gave rise to what has been called the "literature of crisis," beginning with Spengler's *Decline of the West*. Today, we are witnessing the collapse of this civilization, a collapse that is documented by the writings of Fromm, not to speak of the despairing existentialism of Camus and Sartre. There will come a time when the Maoist, believing that the antinomies of western society have been avoided—and perhaps having really avoided them in the economic and social spheres—will find himself or herself face to face with the same question about the ultimate end and meaning of it all.

This will be the time for dialog not between West and East, between capitalism and Maoist Communism, but between a materialistic view of life that has produced its best results in Mao's China, and a transcendent, spiritual view of life that finds its fullest expression in Christianity. This will indeed be a dialog. Maoism will show what people are capable of even without grace, or at least without grace received through its ordinary channels; it will also show that of which they are incapable. For its part, Christianity will show to Maoism what it needs in order to be complete, in order to be able to give meaning to its conquests.

This is why it was fitting that a group of Christians should engage in study and reflection on the New China. In the two colloquia of Båstad and Louvain we see a fact of prophetic import, not so much for what was said there, but for the fact that these colloquia were held in the conviction that in a dialog with Maoism, both the Church and New China have much to say to one another. For this reason we also wish to take part in this dialog, in the hopes of making our contribution, and of offering our assessment in aid of those who are asking what meaning the New China can have for the rest of the world, and for God's plan of salvation.

In the present essay, we shall examine such concepts as "salvation" and "the new person," that keep recurring in discussions of the New China. Then we shall pass to a consideration of the role which the New China is playing in the divine plan of salvation, and of the challenge which this presents to Christians. Our sources of information are the Reports of the Colloquia of Båstad and Louvain.

A Christian can only react with joy on the realization of the great economic, political and social progress which has been achieved in China since 1949. The words with which Mao greeted the victory of the revolution were understandable and legitimate. A people with a great culture and a tradition such as perhaps no other people has known—after being humiliated and offended for more than a century—could finally speak of "standing on their own feet."

It is not only the political independence finally won by the Chinese people which should give Christians reason for satisfaction. What they most appreciate is that, in that immense country, the scourges of hunger, floods, and technical backwardness have been conquered. Whoever has recently visited China after having known it before 1949 cannot help but feel that this is a different country in which it is difficult to recognize the pre-revolutionary one. Even China's international prestige should please a Christian, since it is right that a people of 800 million inhabitants should have their part in the family of nations.

Along with a feeling of joy, a Christian cannot help but nurture a feeling of regret for what the Western, Catholic and Protestant nations have done against China in the last century. It is sufficient to remember the infamous opium war. This was a dark chapter which does no honor to those who were in any way responsible for it. Naturally, the Christian nations did not act as Christians since neither the Gospel nor its morality could back their behavior. In the people's feelings, nevertheless, it was difficult to distinguish the Christian nations from Christianity. The witness of the former showed what the latter probably was. From this came the Chinese aversion for a religion that they could not easily disassociate from western imperialism.

However, these considerations concern the political and historical aspects of New China. Our interest is rather with the religious aspect. It is with this aspect that the Båstad and the Louvain colloquia were concerned. Thus, we ask ourselves: Is a dialog possible between Christianity and the New China? What is the role which the New China is called to play in the plan of salvation?

The Relativity of Theology

This problem seems out of place to some. For a dialog

there must be at least two parties. Now the fact is that China does not want to have anything to do with a dialog and, what is more, she doesn't believe she needs it. She believes she can realize alone that "new person" which has been and is the ideal of Christianity. This fact seems so decisive that some Protestant theologians felt obliged to rethink salvation in a secular context like the Chinese one. We shall briefly report the opinions of two participants in the Båstad colloquium: Raymond Whitehead and Choan-seng Song.

Whitehead, taking off from the fact that "the Chinese revolution has been a genuine movement of social and spiritual liberation based on a secular philosophy which is critical of religion, including Christianity," asks himself if this does not lead us to affirm "the relativity of Christian experience and theology."[1] On the basis of this principle, he raises some questions. Are "God, Jesus and the resurrection" necessary elements of a Christian vision of the world? Can Christians properly think of "the world" in situations which do not include these three realities? Then Whitehead raises another question: If every experience of liberation is incomplete, might not all theoretical expressions of the meaning of this liberation be incomplete? In fact, does Christianity have a partial truth to offer the New China or the "exclusive, ultimate and absolute" truth? And, finally, if the relativity of Christian expressions of salvation are affirmed, is there the possibility of a dialog between Christianity and New China?[2]

After raising these questions, the author returns to the Chinese revolution and indicates its positive and negative sides. It is now more perfect than revolution is in other communities. "What China needs, however, is not liberal values or 'Christianity' as such. An expansion of the community of believers in China would not somehow bring about a new level of liberation there. . . . There is room to learn from each other."[3]

We, Christians, can learn from China "a theology of struggle" which includes a radical rejection of liberal humanism, admits the reality of the class struggle, assigns violence and creative hate to their place, and recognizes that "sometimes revolutionary struggle is the only path to a situation where genuine reconciliation will be possible."[4] Finally, the author says, "In a theology of struggle, human nature and universal love will also be seen from the point of view of struggle."[5] Thus love will be a concept of the future and will be born from the elimination of classes.

Here then is what Christians can learn from Maoism. The author admits the difficulty which arises from the Christian concepts of grace and the cross. But he thinks that a secular concept of Christianity meets the difficulty. Basically, he argues, grace is our faith that the class struggle will succeed, a confidence that has been given to us. Therefore, this faith is a sign of grace. And the same can be said of the cross. This means that for the oppressed of this world we pour ourselves out in order to fight for them. To identify ourselves with them we take on the form of slaves. "The cross," Whitehead concludes, "is a sign of hope and struggle, of resurrection and insurrection."[6]

As we can see, such a dialog between Christianity and Maoism requires, basically, an acceptance of the ideas and practices of Maoism—at least of the class struggle as Mao has conceived it and with which he liberated China. It means renouncing everything in Christianity which might impede participation in this struggle (such as love for one's enemies and nonviolence). But, the reader asks, does Maoism have something to learn from Christianity? Whitehead fails to give an answer to this question. The dialog is one-way. Christianity has nothing "ultimate or absolute" to say to the New China. The Christian concept of salvation is relative. Maoism has achieved a liberation such as no other community has ever done. This is the proof of its truth.

Song's Interpretation

Choan-seng Song tries to define what may be the meaning of the New China in salvation history. "Do we have in New China a challenge to the gospel of salvation as this gospel has been interpreted, developed and propagated by western forms of

Christian faith? And if so, then in what way?[7] It is a problem
that interests us, because China believes that it has "formed a
new system of values which makes religion superfluous." That
role hitherto played by the western nations in the name of the
Bible now seems destined to be played by China in the name of
Socialism. It is possible that a new history will be formed in
which the Exodus will be represented by Mao's "Long March."
We must ask ourselves if the New China will take over in the
history of the world "the role which ancient Israel has played
for the past millenia."[8] We cannot be sure of this, Song argues.
But the problem should be raised.

All of this represents an "embarrassing problem," as the
author recognizes, for such western theology as Cullman's
which does not recognize any role for the so-called non-Christian nations in a salvation history that is made up only by Old
and New Testament happenings. Nevertheless, could God's plan
which is unfolded in Israel and in the Church be only "a model
or type of God's salvation"? Could salvation become incarnate
in varied degrees of intensity and concentration in other nations
and peoples? Song feels he can answer affirmatively. Salvation
history is present and at work in all nations throughout the
events of their history. These are saving in themselves, even if
they are not related to the *Heilsgeschichte.* This means that salvation history is not to be confused with "western cultural or
even moral values."[9] Song then draws on Schubert Ogden.
Some events of history, in order to be saving, ought to manifest
God's action as creator and redeemer. For this end they need
not be supernatural. Saving facts and words can be found everywhere and at all times. Man must know how to read beyond
these facts and words. It is the incapacity to read beyond these
happenings that has not permitted neo-Orthodox theologians to
decipher "the handwriting on the walls of Asian politics."[10] The
moment has come to reinterpret the meaning of history in a new
and more complex context. In dealing with the New China
"Christian theology will need a set of new biblical and theological assumptions that will provide fresh insights into the acts of
God in the extra-biblical histories."[11]

Song applies these principles to the New China. Its importance, he says, lies in wanting to give ultimate meaning to humanity and history and, in this way, in replacing every other truth relative to people and the world. What the New China plans to do will affect not only "human society but human beings." It may fail somewhat, but the socialist movement which struggles for the right of the oppressed will go forward and "China will continue to be a major physical and spiritual force behind the movement."[12]

It is at this point that a link can be made between the New China and salvation history. "Salvation history in the sense of God's act in history is intensely acted out in the transition of the Old China to the New China and in the continuing effort of the Chinese Communist Party to transform man and his society."[13] But while in the Bible this redemptive effort is seen in a religious context, in the New China it is seen in a secular one. "What we have in China," Song continues, "is a secularized version of salvation history. It is no less salvation history even though its basic ideological thrust is that of atheistic materialism." ". . . She [i.e., the New China] is a telling example of how man can do without a hypothesis called God or a *deus ex machina*. In the hands of the Chinese Communist Party, the land of many Gods and many lords has been completely desacralized." Traditional religions, it is true, have suffered from this, including Christianity. On the other hand, the "New China has thus emerged as a formidable spiritual force and institution contesting for supremacy against other spiritual forces and institutions represented by the time-honored great world religions."[14] "This bears a strong stamp of the prophetic activity in the Bible," the author continues. The prophets had a clear social vision but they were not revolutionaries. Jesus, himself, with his message brought a strong revolutionary charge to the world. But western theology has spiritualized it so much as to alienate this message from its origins and turn it into a support of the capitalist system. Thus, when the New China said no to capitalism it did not say no to the Gospel but to western theology which had become aligned with capitalism. It is in the light of Christ and not western theology that we can begin to see "the profound meaning of God's acts in the New China."[15] Under

Mao's impulse she has found a way "to shape the destiny of a nation or even of the world for the welfare of the majority of people"[16]

But then Song asks: "Is New China the Kingdom of God realized?" No, he says, and Mao himself would deny it. In China we have the tension between the "already" and the "not yet," the future of hope "at once realized and suspended in the present."[17] In China there is a struggle for power, a cult of personality. This stops us from saying that she is the kingdom of God even in its secularized version.

This discussion naturally brings us to ask ourselves what salvation is. Song does not propose "to discuss in detail the biblical and theological meaning of salvation,"[18] but rather, by seeing it in the light of incarnation, he describes it as "the freedom to be human." This is what God showed us in Jesus Christ. This salvation brings an opening up to God and other people. For this reason there can be no salvation in an authoritarian state which imposes on its members what they should think and say. It is this which is lacking in China. We can only hope that the Chinese masses, who have found liberation from so many evils, may also find liberation in the truth and in God. Song concludes: "All this goes to show that New China, just as other nations in the past and also in the future, is part of the salvation history which begins with the old creation and ends with the new creation. She is therefore an integral part of the creation which, according to the Apostle Paul, 'will be set free from its bondage to decay and obtain the glorious liberty of the children of God'."[19] It goes without saying that this concept of salvation renders useless every missionary effort of the Church, as Song himself recognizes.[20]

What Is Salvation?

Obviously the problem which the theological interpretations given by the Protestant experts raise—and on whose solution all the other problems depend, above all that of evangelization—lies in the meaning that is given to the words "salvation" and "liberation" by the participants in the colloquium. Song, as we saw a moment ago, refuses to discuss the problem "on a biblical and theological level." And yet the whole question turns on the meaning which is given to the word salvation in the Bible and in theology. Our answer will determine whether a dialog is possible between Christianity and the New China. Therefore, it is of fundamental importance to establish precisely the meaning of the term used and to establish it in a biblical and theological sense. Otherwise, it will no longer be a matter of dialog between the New China and Christianity. Either Christianity is biblical or it isn't Christianity.

What, then, does the term "salvation" mean? As is well-known, "salvation" is one of the key terms of the Bible. To be saved means to be taken away from a more or less serious peril in which there is danger of succumbing. For this to happen, one needs someone stronger than oneself, a savior. In the Old Testament salvation was understood in a largely material way and only slowly acquired the spiritual sense we find in the New Testament. Thus, it is said that God saves the children of Jacob through Joseph (Genesis 45,5), he saves Lot's wife (Wisdom 16,6), he saves Noah from the flood (Wisdom 10,4; see Genesis 7,23), and his people from slavery in Egypt (Exodus 14,13). Once they were led into the promised land, he saves them from their enemies through King Saul (1 Samuel 11,13), David (2 Samuel 3,18) and judges like Samson (Judges 2,16,18) and Gideon (Judges 6,14). Israel knows that God is its Savior and in moments of danger turns to him (Jeremiah 4,14) but complains if the salvation it asks for comes late (Jeremiah 8,20).

Naturally, the need for salvation emerges especially in difficult situations such as the Babylonian captivity. In these cases, salvation assumes an eschatological dimension; it is projected into a future when the situation of danger in which the individual or people find themselves will be over. For Jeremiah, a prophet of the period of exile, God will save his people by leading them again to the land of their fathers (Jeremiah 31,7). Ezekiel asks God to save his sheep by giving them a good pasture (Ezekiel 34,32). Salvation is the fundamental act of God's victorious justice (Isaiah 63,1), which he will send his servant to accomplish (Isaiah 49,6-8). Slowly the concept of salvation becomes universalized. God saves all those who invoke his name (Joel 3,5), all those whose names are written in his book (Daniel 12,1). Wisdom describes for us the salvation of the just on the last day (5,2). The believer is certain that, if God is invoked, he will come to one's aid. In particular, God hears the prayer of the poor (Psalms 34,7), the humble (18,28), the little ones (116,6), the persecuted (55,17), the afflicted hearts (34,19) and, in general, all those who fear him (145,19).

In this way the Bible prepares the people for a more profound concept of salvation which will be found in the New Testament. Here it is not only corporal salvation which God grants through Christ, as occurs with the sick who turn to him (Matthew 9,21; Mark 3,4) and for the disciples struck by the storm (Matthew 8,25; 14,30), but—above all—salvation from sin. Such salvation comes to the sinful woman (Luke 7,48ff.) and to Zacchaeus (Luke 9,56). The mission of Jesus is to save what was lost, to save and not to condemn (John 3,17). He calls himself the door through which one enters into salvation (John 10,9), the good shepherd who has come to save his sheep (Matthew 15,24), who will not get lost if they join his flock (John 10,28; 6,39). On the other hand, in order to be saved, one must lose oneself, yet he who accepts losing himself will have eternal life (Matthew 10,39). Jesus subjects even himself to this law and affirms that he has come for this purpose (John 12,27). In order to have salvation, one must follow him even that far.

After the resurrection, the apostles preach that Jesus is the Savior authenticated by God (Acts 5,31), that in no other name is it possible to be saved (4,12). People are called to believe in order to be saved (2,40). This faith is the condition for salvation (16,30-31). It is salvation from sin that is obtained through repentance and baptism, as Peter affirms on Pentecost day (2,38) before the Sanhedrin (3,19) and to Cornelius (10,43).

St. Paul and the Pauline tradition develop these ideas and give us an early theological synthesis of salvation. For the apostle, God desires the salvation of all (1 Timothy 2,4). For this he sent his Son on earth showing in him the love which he brings to humanity (Titus 2,11). In fact, by dying for us, Christ became "the prince of eternal salvation" (Hebrews 5,19), and Savior of his mystical body (Ephesians 5,23). Therefore, the Gospel which announces his message is "the power of God for salvation to everyone who has faith" (Romans 1,16). The apostle also announces this has no other goal than the salvation of all (1 Corinthians 9,22), Hebrews and pagans alike.

Nevertheless, the salvation which the Gospel gives us, which is conferred in baptism, the sacrament of rebirth (John 3,5) which makes us children of God and heirs of eternal life (Hebrews 1,14) and justifies us (Romans 5,1) gives all this to us but only in hope (Romans 8,24). That is, although salvation is already possessed, it gives us the right to an inheritance which will not be revealed until the end of time (1 Peter 1,5), when, since we are already justified and reconciled in Christ's blood, we will be saved by him from God's wrath (Romans 5,9ss). Christ himself will appear to give us salvation (Hebrews 9,28). The Christian lives in expectation of that day when Christ will complete his work by transforming our body (Philippians 3,20-21). In this sense salvation is the object of hope (Romans 8,23ff.). Then we will be delivered from everything that can mar our happiness, such as sickness, suffering, death and all those evils from which the psalmist asked to be liberated and which Jesus overcame with his miracles by giving us a sample of the total liberation which would come about only at the end. This will be the final victory of God and Christ (Apocalypse 7,10).[21]

Salvation and Liberation

From the texts which we have rapidly cited, it can be seen that, according to the Bible, salvation embraces two dimensions. The first, commonly called "liberation," consists of the elimination of all individual and social, physical and moral evils which can hinder people from the full development of their personality, their energies and their potential. The most terrible of all these evils—the one which conditions human liberation from the others—is undoubtedly death. This is the end, the return to nothingness. In the face of this, one cannot help but ask what meaning life has, what meaning there is in the struggle and possible victory against all individual and social, physical and moral evils. It is the problem which in all eras has provoked human reflection and which, at times, has forced people to confess the inability to give an answer, or at least one that could satisfy the heart. Next to death, the evil which, more than the others, threatens a human being, inasmuch as it can make one ineffective and useless, is loneliness. People are made to live in community and only there can they find the possibility of perfecting themselves and of developing their own potential. It is a fact, however, that this desire crashes against the wall of loneliness which is effectively described by so much modern literature. Each person is a mystery. One feels made for other people but doesn't succeed in communicating with them. There is no real liberation without overcoming these two evils, death and loneliness, which theology calls "sin." They find their historical origin in that original sin by which people grew far from God and lost both the gift of immortality which God had granted and the gift of dialog with him which they had possessed until that time. Humans are destined for dialog with God and then with other persons. When through disobedience contact with God was lost, the individual became an enigma to self and others. Each one saw the subjection to death; while feeling made for life. Each felt the difficulty of communicating with others— the one, who in dialog with others, could have found full self-development. Here, then, is what is usually called the negative element of salvation or liberation. Liberation, we repeat, is liberation from those evils which hinder humans from being themselves or, as Song says, from being "fully human."

There is also the positive dimension which is more often called "salvation" and which the Bible also calls "justification" (Romans 8,30; 3,24, etc.). This consists of participation in divine life, in becoming "adopted children of God." Jesus came on earth so that we might receive this adoption. As the apostle puts it, in the fullness of time God sent his Son on earth "so that we might receive adoption as sons" (Galatians 4,5). It is this filiation which allows us to turn to God and call him "Father," something which is impossible without the action of the

Holy Spirit in our hearts (Galatians 4,6-7). This adoption comes about through a rebirth "of water and the Holy Spirit" (John 3,5). This is a new creation, an internal transformation for the individual, who is born as a slave but becomes a child with the right to God's heredity. The apostle says: "So through God you are no longer a slave but a son, and if a son then an heir" (Galatians 4,7). It is to make this adoption possible that Christ died by reconciling us with the Father and readmitting us into his friendship. By dying and rising he conquered death and re-opened the path toward the Father, granting us victory over death and loneliness. But even though all of this is actually conferred on us in baptism, which draws its efficacy from faith in Christ, it will find its complete fulfillment "in the future age." Then the dead will rise up to take part in the inheritance promised to them as sons and daughters of God.

Salvation's Two Components

In Christian salvation, there are two components: one horizontal, and the other vertical. The first, which we have called liberation, can be seen either as a presupposition to or a consequence of the second one. Liberation from material, individual and social evils can either prepare people for their meeting with God or be the consequence of it. In general, we can say that these two components go together. Although Jesus refused to be a temporal and political Messiah, as many of his peers expected, and stated openly that his kingdom was not of this world (John 18,36), nevertheless, he did not give the kingdom he preached an exclusively spiritual character. Thus the word *sozein* in the New Testament is often used to indicate the material healing which Jesus performed. This appears when he cured two blind men. They approached him and said to him: "Have mercy on us Son of David." When he entered the house he asked them: "Do you believe that I am able to do this?" When they answered yes, he replied: "According to your faith be it done to you." In that moment their eyes opened (Matthew 9, 27-30). Jesus first forgave the sins of the paralytic who asked to be healed (Matthew 9,2), which provoked the Pharisees' disdain. This is a clear sign that for Jesus, material healing could accompany spiritual healing. The two go together even if not necessarily so. In the same way we also see Jesus ignoring the prejudices of his age and approaching any person or social group, in order to show that for him there were no distinctions based on a person's ethnic or social origin. So he dealt with Samaritans, tax-gatherers (publicans), an adulteress, prostitutes, lepers, pagans, with those who today are called "marginalized." For him all men were brothers, and women sisters, since they were children of the same Father who is in heaven and who makes his sun shine on all without discrimination (Matthew 5,45).

We can see that for Jesus it is the vertical dimension, humanity's relationship with God, their being children of the same Father, which abolishes everything that creates distinctions and discrimination among them. For him all are equal, because they have the same origin and are called to the same destiny. For Paul, too, there is no distinction of "Greek and Jew, circumcised and uncircumcised, barbarian, Scythian, slave, free person, but Christ is all, and in all" (Colossians 3,11). He goes much further than this and tells us that the salvation won for us by Christ extends even to nature, which waits with eager longing for "the revealing of the sons of God" (Romans 8,19).

In this way, salvation understood in its vertical dimension gives the Christian a completely new perspective with which to see other people and natural things. It really gives a total vision of history and humanity. All history is directed toward realizing this unity among people; making them one people, the people of God, which begins its march in this world and will conclude at the end of time when there will be "a new heaven and a new earth" (2 Peter 3,13). During the course of the centuries, the Church held to this teaching by trying to keep these two components of salvation united as much as she could. In this regard it is sufficient to read the description of Christian life left to us by the apologist Aristides[22] and the letter to Diognetus.[23] But it took centuries before the Church realized all the implications of salvation. Even St. Paul, for whom neither slave nor freeman existed, sent the slave Onesimus back to his master, Philemon, and only asked that he treat him as he himself would have treated him.

The New Christian Man

From the concept of salvation, as we have set it forth, there follows the biblical vision of the new humanity—an important concept, if not the main one, which comes up in literature regarding the New China and its relations with Christianity.

According to the Bible, the "new humanity" is the justified humanity—the saved who have accepted Christ's redemption through faith and the sacrament of baptism in which we are "reborn" (John 3,5). The old one has been cast off and replaced by the new one who is made in Christ's image, the perfect being in whom God showed why humanity was called and how he wanted it to be. Because of Adam's sin, humankind had become a "slave of sin" (Romans 6,6,17). But Christ, with his death and resurrection, renewed and regenerated humanity in order to make it different from what it had been before—a "new humanity," no longer formed in the image of Adam from whom it was descended, but in the image of Christ by whom it was redeemed and remade. Christ is the new Adam who gives life to all (Corinthians 15,22) so that after his redemption all men and women become one in him (Colossians 3,11). The Christian, therefore, whom Christ regenerates in baptism, can be called the "workmanship of God" (Ephesians 2,10). In baptism one becomes a part of Christ and can be called "a new creation," for "the old has passed away, behold, the new has come" (2 Corinthians 5,17). After baptism "neither circumcision counts for anything nor uncircumcision," that is, neither pagan nor Hebrew but only "a new creation" (Galatians 6,16).

Such a profound transformation which is effected in us can only come about through the intervention of the Spirit (Romans 7,6; Galatians 5,16-25). It works in baptism and grows through our knowledge of the word of God (1 Peter 2,2), the truth which in us effects justice (Ephesians 4,24) and faith (Galatians, 5,5-6).

In this way Christians are always more and more renewed, and more and more reproduce the image of him who made them (Colossians 3,10), and grow until they become mature "to the measure of the stature of the fullness of Christ" (Ephesians 4,13).

This concept of the new humanity must have immediate repercussions on the life of the Christian who considers God as Father and all human beings as brothers and sisters, loving them according to the Savior's precept and taking part in their joys and sorrows by feeling part of their destiny which is identical with his or her own. The Church is precisely the community of the saved, of those reborn in Christ, the sons and daughters of God who love one another and await the day when they will be able to take part in the inheritance which they already possess but which is not yet revealed fully.

Chinese Liberation and Christian Salvation

From what we have said so far, a fundamental fact emerges for those who deal with relations between Christianity and the New China: the liberation which Mao has accomplished or is accomplishing in his country does not match an integral view of Christian salvation. The great economic and social victories achieved by Chinese Communism are certainly part of human liberation. For this, as Christians, we rejoice with those who were its builders. The victory over evils arising from such natural calamities as floods, the improvement of public health through medicine, the disappearance of social differences, rising standards of living, the elimination of the evils of prostitution and alcoholism—all these are undoubtedly signs of a liberation prefigured in the miracles of the Gospel.

This liberation, however, cannot be complete. Apart from the fact that a Christian cannot accept the violence and hate used to effect this liberation, the Chinese Revolution, like any other revolution, has failed and could only fail in the most important point—in the liberation from death. Neither Mao nor any other revolutionary has ever seriously hoped to achieve this kind of liberation. Still, this is everyone's constant aspiration. What is the point of creating with enormous effort a better society if those who created and enjoyed it will have to disappear one day without any power in the world being able to stop this?

The problem of death, as we all know, is one which Communism does not deal with willingly. For Communism, it is not a relevant question. Marx himself hardly touched the subject. The reason is that, for Marxism, the individual does not exist while class consciousness does exist. The individual renounces "self" for class consciousness. The problem of death exists for one who is still conscious of "self," of being a person "unto oneself." If one admits that what exists is class, then the problem disappears. A recent Marxist thinker, Ernst Bloch, says: "Immortality is radically realized by man himself and it is never present as a mythological fact. Revolutionary consciousness has something of immortality: the immortality of the best in man's intentions and makeup."[24]

We, Christians, frankly are not satisfied with this collective immortality; it seems an escape from the terrible problem which death represents for humanity. We admit, and readily, that there may be, or rather that there are people—and Communism has had many—who are willing to die for an ideal, ready to sacrifice themselves for a better world, for a more just society, even at the cost of disappearing into nothingness. But when this better world has finally begun, when all can enjoy the good things that this world places at the disposal of people freed from all servitude, the problem of death remains intact. Can a life be really enjoyed which offers every possible pleasure but which is destined to end? A. Schaaf expresses this problem very well when he asks, "The question remains on the lips of one who is tired of life's trials and disappointments: What is the good of it? And, above all, there remains the question which comes from reflecting on death: What good is it all if we must die?"[25] Not much can be done: consideration after consideration can be lined up about class consciousness, but each one lives the death of a loved one as a real, terrible and disturbing fact. "Is life then worth living?" one asks.[26] It is useless: until Marxism answers this problem, it will not have realized humanity's true liberation, because it will not have freed it from its greatest "serviture."

Bloch perceived the problem and tried to answer it. He noted very well how the "social" aspect of death, that is, the part connected with the exploitation of men and women, will be definitely eliminated by Socialism. But he immediately added that there is another aspect to death, the "natural one," which is beyond "the solution of the social problem" and which does not arise until after the social problem has been solved. When there is nothing left to fight for, when humanity has opened up the infinite possibilities which a just society puts at its disposal, it will feel more than ever death's intrusion into life, since it will come to cut off these possibilities. No ending could be so bitter and absurd. At the most beautiful moment, life is taken away from us! And then, is it worth living? Bloch writes: "Not only is the cadaver pale; but dynamism is impoverished and belittled, because of death. The tomb, darkness, putrefaction, worms—if they are not removed, they have had and continue to have a restraining and depreciating force."[27]

In the face of "natural" death the social death of the Communist hero who sacrificed himself for the building of a better society becomes meaningless. Was it worthwhile to fight so much, sacrifice one's life for the creation of a society that is incapable of eliminating its worst enemy? Bloch is correct in saying that death is the great "non-utopia."[28] He asks himself, and we with him, why Marxists have given so little space to death in their thinking when it is so basic. He suggests that this neglect is due to the fact that men and women have continued unconsciously to live "in a religious hope hidden behind death or he has secularized this hope in the expectations of a Communist paradise coming from this earth."[29] Yet this position cannot be sustained. Death is an inescapable fact and the remembrance of heroes who died for the cause means nothing, if we consider that the human species is destined for extinction. Bloch does not feel like accepting such a bitter perspective and he opens his heart to hope. "No one knows," he says, "if the life process doesn't contain or allow some transformation even if invisible."[30]

This is the real problem which the New China will soon have to face. If Mao's revolution has really been successful, it will find itself even sooner before this problem in all its acuteness. For its part, Christianity maintains it has the answer and a complete answer, which not only satisfies the Socialist person but does justice to all those who have struggled in order for him/her to exist. It is the doctrine of the resurrection from the dead, guaranteed by Christ's own resurrection.

The Vertical Dimension

If the Chinese and Christian versions of liberation reveal some analogies regarding the horizontal dimension of salvation which we noted in the preceding pages, there are none regarding the vertical dimension—which is far more important and, in fact, the basis of the first dimension. Salvation consists essentially of participating in divine life, in God's adoptive filiation which takes place in us through faith and baptism and is expressed in the exercise of the three theological virtues of faith, hope and charity.

We do not doubt that in China there may be those, Christian or otherwise, who live these three virtues and who, in one way or another, have found God and given themselves to him even without knowing it exactly. The human soul is made for God and will not find peace until it rests in him. And this is also true for the Chinese soul. There is no doubt that this encounter with God is facilitated by the social education imparted in the New China. The need to think of others, to think in function of others, to cooperate with others in the establishment of a more just society must lead the Chinese in ever-growing numbers to practice these virtues and express the charity which Jesus indicated in his eschatological discourse. Whoever works for others, gives them to eat and drink, cures their ills, wards off the danger which can threaten their safety, in fact works for all people, who have divine vocations, and thus in some way works for God who created humanity and wants all to love one another.

But if this suffices to let us believe that in China there are many "anonymous" Christians, that is, who are Christians without knowing it, this doesn't allow us to say that China is a Christian country to the point that they no longer need the Gospel preached by missionaries, since it has arrived in China through Marxism and is often liable to a secularized interpretation like Whitehead's or Song's. To state that salvation can be accomplished without "God, Christ and the resurrection" means placing oneself outside Christianity, which maintains that God sent his Son on earth so that all who believe in him would not perish but have eternal life (John 3,15). A Christianity that lacks God, Christ and the resurrection is not Christianity: it is not a message of salvation.

Herein lies our disagreement with those who believe that a "secularized version" of Christianity is complete. Although the New China may be a type of humanism, perhaps even a particularly successful humanism, it is not a type of Christianity. Although there might be a book entitled "Existentialism is a humanism" or "Atheism is a humanism," there can be no book entitled "Christianity is a mere humanism." If someone should study such a title, he/she ought to have the honesty to admit that the Christianity spoken of is not the Bible's.

It is a fact, nonetheless, that many persons after having visited China do not hesitate to say that there are "Christian values" there. Even the *Fides* agency recognized this in a report of April 4, 1973. There we read: "Present-day China has tended toward a mystique of disinterested work in the service of others, toward an aspiration for justice, an exaltation of the simple and frugal life, an elevation of the peasant masses and a mix of social classes. Is this not precisely what is said and re-said incomparably in the encyclicals *Pacem in Terris* and *Populorum Progressio* as well as in the 1971 Synod document "Justice in the World"? The formation of a community consciousness is learned today from the Chinese. But is this not precisely what Vatican Council II repeatedly asked of the People of God?"[31]

All of this is true, but it is not enough to say that Christianity exists in China. For inasmuch as it may be a carrier of values, even humanity's highest values, Christianity is essentially a person-Christ, the Word become flesh for man's salvation. There is no Christianity without Christ and without that vertical dimension of his message which points to the salvation coming from God as a gift. Chinese Communism aims at the here and now. For Christianity, the kingdom of God, even though it begins here, will only have its fulfillment and total perfection in the community of the risen, in eternal life, in the definitive and total encounter of God and man. So if we can speak of Christian values present and functioning in China, we cannot speak of Christianity being there. Christianity is essentially transcendental; the New China is essentially terrestrial.

The New Man

Neither can we confuse the new person of Christianity with the new human being that Chinese Communism intends to create in the New China. The fundamental difference between the two concepts lies in their relationship to transcendence. We noted that in our discussion of salvation. The new Christian is the one reborn by baptism in Christ's image who lives from faith, hope and charity, and who "by growing in charity reaches the stature of Christ." This will take place fully only in eternal life. The new Christian is ready to die for others and to renounce everything which is in opposition to the divine vocation.

The new Chinese is placed on another plane. He/she is a person formed through sacrifice and abnegation in order to place the whole self at the disposal of others. If all of this is worthy of admiration and coincides in many ways with the Christian's behavior, the Chinese individual is, nevertheless, lacking that "something" which would lead to one's becoming the new person as the Bible intends. Lacking would be the "spiritual rebirth," which would put one in a position to act no longer as a mere individual, but as "a son of God." It can be added that the Christian man or woman is "in himself or herself" an already complete reality, even if in order to develop and reach maturity there is need for society and the contribution of equals to whom one gives and from whom one receives. For

Marxism, the person is something coming into being which eventually dissolves and disappears into society. These are very different concepts, even philosophically.

But if this is so, how can we explain that the Chinese individual knows how to live for others? The answer lies in humanity's social nature. Communism knew how to develop this with careful education and gave us a person who was "new" with respect to the pre-revolutionary Chinese (who was largely concerned with his/her interests, his/her "daily rice"), but not "new" in the sense that there was a different nature than before. For Christians, the new individual is not a renovated old one but one in whom the old one is eliminated. He/she is let die in order that a new creature can function through God's intervention. This new one can lack everything on a material level, but still enjoy a certain liberty of spirit which even the wealthiest person in the world does not possess. He/she can realize himself and herself despite the state of slavery to which they may be externally subjected. Even though the slave-Christian of the early centuries was deprived of freedom and many other things, that individual did not feel less free or less of a man or woman than the master who considered the person a "thing." Instead that person could feel superior to him, because in possession of that "something" which made one a "child of God" and a participant in a reality and a destiny which no human power would have been able to give or take away. It is a new perspective which reveals in others not only an equal to whom one is bound by a solidarity based on common nature and social status, but a brother or sister belonging to a very special community, the Church, the people of God on earth, the temple of the Spirit to whom one is attached by the ties of love and not only those of justice.

But if all of this is true, why do so many people have the impression that in China there is a new humanity, so that they can say that China is the only Christian country in the world? It seems that this impression carries the observers' judgment beyond the realm of experience to that of theology. When faced with what one sees in Christian countries, it is easy to conclude that the Gospel may be practiced in China and not in Christian countries. These observers are very often not theologians. They can easily pick up a Christian expression about "the new humanity" and apply it in the same sense to Chinese Communism. This is a mistake into which it is easy to fall. This observation brings us now to the main problem: What place does the New China have in the divine plan of salvation?

The New China and the Plan of Salvation

J. Charbonnier and L. Trivière attempt to answer this question in their paper at Båstad[32] in which they take up a traditional church doctrine. We are not in fact dealing with a problem which has been posed for the first time today by the New China. It came up when Christianity spread through the Roman Empire. The messengers of the Gospel were asked by the pagans: Why had Christ come so late, if he were the true Savior of humankind?

The answer was already outlined by St. Paul in his discourse on the Areopagus when he spoke to the representatives of pagan learning. They did not put any problem to him; they only wanted to know what the "new thing" was that he was teaching. Recalling an inscription he had happened to read on a column dedicated to "the unknown God," Paul stated that he wished to announce to the Athenians that very God whom they were seeking but did not know (Acts 17,23). There is profound intuition in this expression which is valid for all times, and which in all times can provide theologians with the principles for seeing and evaluating God's presence in history, his work in realizing the plan to admit humanity into communion with him and make them into one people, the people of God. Paul speaks of the "ages of ignorance" (Acts 17,30) of God in which humanity lived while God awaited the right moment to reveal himself to them in his fullness. But even in these times of "ignorance" God did not abandon people by being indifferent to them. He displayed his presence with signs which were accessible to everyone and from which they could come to know his action and his providence. These signs are the very works of creation from which we can know God and through which he shows that he is close to us. In the Letter to the Romans, St. Paul states that this way of knowing God was effective because it was from his creatures that the pagans knew God and his providence (Romans 1,19ff.). It is clearly an imperfect knowledge (1 Corinthians 13,12), but one sufficient for people to know that above them there is a Being which governs all things. The apostle further speaks of the history of nations, to each of which God allotted in space and time the "boundaries of their habitation" (Acts 17,26). And all of this was to give humankind the possibility to seek God and "find him."

On the basis of these principles, we can say that all that humanity has done in history and all that continues to occur in history is destined in God's plan to prepare the encounter between him and his creatures which was to take place in Jesus Christ. In this sense we can accept what Ogden and Song maintain. Salvation history and the events which comprise it are not limited to the Old and New Testament, but are spread through the whole of history. Naturally the facts of the Old and particularly of the New Testament have a very special value. They cannot be put on the same level as the events of so-called "secular history." But this "privilege" is not so exclusive as to take away all value from the events of ordinary history. We can easily say that in every nation certain people and events have enjoyed a particular importance which let them glimpse that presence and action of God which were to be fully revealed in Jesus Christ. We can attribute a certain prophetic role to the great founders of religions and admit that a special providence has been displayed in them. In God's plan they were destined to nurture with their thinking the lives of millions of people called by God to salvation. In some way, at least, we can say the same regarding the historical events which took place around them and determined their culture and sensitivity. Through these events they were moved to pose the great problems of humanity's origin and destiny. In this sense such events were "saving," even if their interpretation was not guaranteed by biblical inspiration as were the events of the two Testaments.

Vatican II's declaration, *Nostra Aetate*, in speaking of

those who belong to various religions, states that they expect from these religions "the answer to the hiden enigmas of the human condition which yesterday as today perturb man's heart."[33] What this statement says about religions can also be applied to *all* historical facts, albeit in a lesser degree. It can be applied, for instance, to philosophical research and—in general —to all those facts which express mankind's spiritual dimension. Whoever thinks will be faced with these problems. The facts of history, understood as a succession of events like wars, the great migrations of peoples and the progress of science, all have the same goal: to stop human beings from sinking into the dullness of everyday life by forcing them to think, to raise questions and find answers for themselves.

The New China

If then all the events of history contain a plan and message from God, what is the message which he is giving us through the great achievements of the New China?

In our opinion, this message is twofold. First of all, God wants to show us what humanity is capable of achieving even without him, or—rather—without an explicit knowledge or recognition of him and his grace. China's great victories, in fact, have been carried out without God or, rather, through a conscious rejection of him in the conviction that people do not need God for their liberation. One can be a "new person" through one's own power. In order to conquer age-old evils one can do without God. A just society can emerge through the effort of a whole nation which officially declares itself to be atheist. Unselfishness, sharing in the destiny of others and a spirit of sacrifice can exist even outside Christianity. A new social order can be founded on mere "natural law," if we may use an expression which Chinese Communism would reject, but which has a very specific meaning for us in that we recognize God's voice in its dictates.

As many speakers at Båstad and Louvain state, this is a fact which leads theologians to rethink some affirmations which have been made perhaps on the basis of principles grounded in revelation, but applied without the necessary discrimination. Experience is a source of awareness for everyone. It can never be left aside and can lead to seeing in a different light what was previously believed to be certain. The same phenomenon is taking place for the New China which took place at the time of the great geographical discoveries. Some virtuous people created the myth of the "noble savage." Theologians asked how these noble savages who lacked grace could keep the precepts of natural law. It was common doctrine that original sin made this impossible, at least in the long haul. This impression faded away quickly, either because it was discovered that the savages were less virtuous than was believed at first, or because it was not difficult to extend even to them the principle of grace's universality and its communication even beyond the ordinary channels used by the Church. A problem still comes up about the faith necessary for salvation (Hebrews 11,6), its content, and the point in time in which it can be said that the Gospel was promulgated for each and every nation and person.

Leaving aside these more technical problems, let us emphasize again the message which comes to us from the New China: people can do good even if they reject God. Provided one finds oneself in a position in which it is impossible to know God or know him properly, one is not responsible for the denial of God. Despite this denial, God will not fail to communicate his grace to whoever tries to do as much as one can in order to live according to the principles of conscience. These principles do not seem unknown to Mao, at least in the positive part of his thinking. The principles stated in Chapter XXVI of the *Little Red Book* are completely acceptable to Catholic morality.[34] Many of God's commandments are reflected there, even if the first and most important one of all is missing. But isn't one who observes God's commandments probably on the way to Christian salvation? Although we have refused to say that Mao's China is a Christian country, we have no difficulty in recognizing that Christian virtues are practiced there, even if they are not exactly the theological virtues of Christianity. Nothing stops those virtues from being found in so many Chinese hearts which God has reached with his grace "through paths known only to him."[35]

The New China, furthermore, as distinct from what took place in Soviet Communism, enjoys the merit of having intuited and emphasized in so many ways that there can be no social change without humanity's interior change. Perhaps unintentionally, Mao opposes the Marxist thesis according to which all human evils come from the society in which one lives so that it is sufficient to change society in order to change people. Mao has intuited that change must come from humanity. New men and women give rise to a new society. What counts above all is their transformation, the basis of all progress.

This is a Christian principle which comes to Mao probably from Confucianism. The fact that he has inculcated it as an indispensable principle shows that he is closer to Christianity than he himself believes. Some intuitions, even if they have found their true depth in Christianity, are inherent in human nature itself.

The Limits of the New China

But if the New China shows what humankind is capable of, even in a society without God, it also shows that of which it is not capable. According to Whitehead, one of the problems which the New China poses for Christianity is that of knowing whether "the Christian who approaches China today has any exclusive, ultimate, absolute truths to proclaim to the Chinese people." The author's answer is negative, although he admits that Christianity is not lacking in "truth" to be proposed to the New China. To us, however, it seems that the problem lies right there and that, with regard to this problem, Maoism falls short. Here is the main gap, the weak point at which Whitehead's thinking stops.

Maoism, as we have said earlier, even though it may have liberated China from the "four old men," has not liberated it from the one we call "the old one *par excellence*," certainly the oldest of all, the one from which we must be liberated if we want the other liberations to have meaning: we refer to death.

Mao praised Comrade Bethune because he gave his life for the Chinese people in the most unselfish way. We join in this praise and admiration. The fact still remains that Comrade Bethune, although he contributed to the victory of the revolution, did not take part in it and, what is more serious, even those who are taking part in it will have to die one day. What meaning, then, attaches to the immense effort made by the Chinese people to establish a more just society, if one day those who have seen the victory must vanish and, with few exceptions, without leaving any trace? The liberation which Mao has given to the Chinese people does not mean much, if he does not also give them this. But he cannot give them this liberation, the most important liberation of all.

The Dialog between Christianity and New China

Therefore, even though the New China continues to reject Christianity and tries to wipe away all traces of Christianity from its land, a dialog between Christianity and Mao's ideology is essential. Christianity is not a political and social system, even though it has had and continues to have deep political and social repercussions. It is essentially a religion of salvation that maintains the incarnation, death and resurrection of the Son of God. This readmits humanity into God's friendship, enabling it to participate in his intimacy and find in the community of salvation, which is the Church, eternal life through the resurrection of the body. It is this which Mao needs in order that the effort made by him and the whole Chinese people may take on its full meaning.

An editor of *Pro Mundi Vita* in the presentation of the Båstad and Louvain colloquia said he could not see how Chinese Communism could tolerate a Roger Garaudy with his *From Anathema to Dialogue* or a Solzhenitsyn.[37] We are not so pessimistic. We believe rather that Chinese Communism will sooner or later produce men and women such as these. If what tourists and journalists describe corresponds to the truth, a Garaudy or Solzhenitsyn is not far off. China, in their opinion, both endorses Christian values and practices such virtues as the dedication to others so well expressed in Mao's article, *Serve the People*. It seems impossible to us that, sooner or later, a man or woman will not cry out and ask why one must love the people and sacrifice oneself for others. If there are already Christian values in China, the problem of their origin must be faced. They are branches broken off from a tree. Sooner or later these branches will miss the tree from which they were broken off.

It is inevitable. Humankind is made to think, to raise problems. And the most important problem is that of the ultimate end, the meaning of history. When the Chinese people will finally become free to think, they will pose this question and, in order for them to have a valid answer, there can only be Christianity. Mao, as we know, has rejected the religion of Christ as a Western element, a residue of imperialism, and we understand his feeling. But when Christianity will cease being seen in this perspective, the Chinese who is no longer conditioned by the past and anti-Western prejudice will ask about the ultimate meaning of things and only Christianity will be able to give an answer.

We go a long way in our optimism. It is not only human nature and reflection that will lead the Chinese to a dialog with Christianity and let them see in it the adequate answer to the problem of history's ultimate meaning which Mao could not give them. We believe that Communism, precisely because it has created a more just society in China, will have prepared the way for Christianity. What indeed does it mean to create a more just society? It means taking away from people the troubles of everyday life, the struggle for existence which afflicts so many nations and human beings. It means creating definitively a society in which the individual is finally free to think, reflect and exercise the higher faculties in complete freedom. And what is a person who reflects if not one who raises the problem of the absolute, the ultimate end?

Furthermore, this is just what has occurred in our Western society. It achieved well-being and some social justice before China did. Once it reached this point, Western society immediately became aware of the shortcomings in a goal which now hardly seemed worth the struggle. The disillusionment which well-being has provoked is enormous and even risks destroying the "consumer" society. When we read Erich Fromm's studies, such as *Psychoanalysis of Contemporary Society* or *Anatomy of Human Destructiveness,* there is enough to be horrified. Certainly it was not this which people expected from a century of progress for which they paid such a high price.

In Western civilization, two tendencies have grown up, two visions of the world: the desperate one of atheist existentialism and the religious search which sees in God, even if only vaguely, the answer to our problems. There is a rebirth of religious sentiment which men and women of science did not foresee but which presents itself to us as the outcome of our needs. Through thinking they realize that they are more than animals and that they have other than material needs. In the West, social progress which did its job through teaching a practical materialism, after having deadened humanity's spiritual aspirations, ended up having to observe that these aspirations were not dead. They burst out again and clamored for an answer more loudly than ever. Even the Marxists who were so sure of the scientific quality of their analysis of history finally had to admit that there were some deep gaps in it. This appears in Bloch's book which we have drawn upon in connection with the problem of death. Max Horkheimer provides us with another example. He ended up confessing to a "nostalgia for the totally Other"—the fear that God did not exist.[38]

If this has happened in Western culture, we have no reason to believe that the same will not occur in the Chinese culture. Even in Chinese Communism, once the intoxication with great achievements passes, the problem will rise of giving meaning to them. This will be the moment for Christianity. The Gospel will appear really as Good News capable of answering the tremendous question which Communism provoked for the Chinese without being able to give a response that could hold up under reflection.

Chinese Communism has assumed the function that the Roman Empire and Greek culture performed for the ancient

Church. These prepared the way for the Gospel by providing a means of expansion and creating a culture which, after magnificent results, fell into decadence and made the need felt for something better. One of the reasons for the spread of the Gospel was the aspiration for ideals higher than those which the prevailing culture could propose. Christianity appeared like fresh air bringing vitality to an exhausted body. The same will happen with Communism. It has already happened to Russian Communism which has given us not only a Solzhenitsyn but the whole movement of religious renewal represented in *samizot*.

In another way the New China is preparing the way for the Gospel: the destruction which it brought about of the "four old men." China has a great culture. Confucianism expresses the Chinese soul in what is uniquely Chinese, but it also shuts off everything that is not Chinese. Communism has the "merit" of having swept away so many political, social and cultural structures which did not allow Christianity to be perceived as Good News. "What do you have to say to us," the 16th and 17th century Chinese asked the Jesuits, "which we do not already know?" They could not admit that foreigners might give them something new. This was a real problem for the missionaries. Now the situation is changed. China accepted a Western ideology which, as everyone recognizes, is rich in Christian values. But it was accepted by Mao, by a man who assimilated it and presented it in a Chinese cultural context. This means that the Chinese today have become more disposed to receiving non-Chinese values, as long as they are presented to them in a way congenial to their own sensibility. This precedent gives some cause for hope. Christianity will be able to appear to the Chinese not as a Western reality but for what it really is—a universal reality. It is a little like Communism. If in so many of its statements and analyses Communism typifies Western culture, it is simply universal in the values which it propagates, such as social justice and the equality of all people. The same holds true for Christianity. Its values are not linked to one culture.

If what tourists and journalists say is true, there are in China Christian values lived by the Chinese people. The Chinese "new humanity" has appeared to many to be like the Christian new humanity. We have argued against this. Yet the fact remains about Christian values being accepted in China. In any dialog between China and Christianity, those values will have to be retraced to their source and be studied in depth, thus transforming human virtues into Christian ones. To express ourselves in terminology which is widely used in modern catechetical literature, we could say that Maoism is effecting pre-evangelization in China.

Is Evangelization Still Up-To-Date?

It seems natural to ask at this point: If Christian values have already been accepted and practiced in China, then does evangelization by the Church still have meaning? Is it still meaningful to speak of China's conversion to Christianity?

Some of the participants at the Båstad and Louvain meetings answered in the negative. Song, for example, in speaking about the interest which the Christian world displays in New China, suspects a missionary concern in this interest and writes: "The assumption that any man or any nation, New China not excepted, can be treated as the object of religious conversion is as missiologically false as biblically untenable. This is the subject which should be basic to any talk on the implication of New China for Christian mission."[39] Rhea Whitehead, in posing the same problem, declares: "In present day Chinese society millions of men and women have achieved a new sense of 'self-actualization' and 'participation in the creation of a community that fosters the becoming of women and men.' What does it mean then to speak of reaching 'others for conversion in Christ'?"[40]

These opinions exclude a mission of the Church in China which could operate in the traditional way and which would make conversion one of its goals. Song believes that the theme of conversion is "biblically untenable." We understand the two authors' thinking. For them, Christianity is nothing more than humanity's liberation, a means for giving each person the possibility of being "completely human" and of "self-realization." In that case, conversion to Christ would not be necessary. If China has really achieved or will achieve liberation, as Song believes, there is no sense to going there and preaching a liberation which they already possess. It makes no sense to convert to Christ these people who have already achieved the self-realization of which the Gospel is supposed to consist. When Christianity is denied a vertical dimension, evangelization loses its whole meaning.

In reality, when the problem of evangelization's relevance to China comes up, the practical question must be distinguished from the theological one. No one believes today that it would be possible to send missionaries to China who would resume an evangelizing work which was interrupted in 1949. The government would not permit it, and perhaps the people themselves would not be willing to listen to a message which could appear to them as a residue of Western imperialism. Time will have to pass before China can see evangelization in its proper light. Even though we believe that Communism is preparing the way for the Gospel, we do not feel that the moment has arrived to take this path. Let us not forget that the *samizot* movement only began in Russia in the last decade. And yet Russia is a country with a Christian background. The moment for China's evangelization has not yet come. Even if the frontiers were opened, the problem would persist.

If, however, we raise the theological question, we believe that, beyond question, China needs evangelization. Christ's mandate to announce the message of salvation to all nations cannot bypass the New China. The Chinese, too, are called to join the people of God which knows no barriers of race or civilization. Even though we are convinced that, as well as a few million baptized Christians, many anonymous Christians exist in China, we are also convinced that this anonymity must cease in order to make room for the full recognition of God's great works which are manifested in Jesus Christ and in the Church, his extension in time and space. Every tongue, says St. Paul, "confesses that Jesus Christ is the Lord to the glory of God the Father" (Philippians 2,11). The mission is the proclamation of the divine plan of salvation, God's revelation. One-fourth of all humanity cannot be excluded from this. How and when this possibility will be opened up for the Church it is impossible to say.

Christians' Task in China

Although evangelization is not yet an actual fact, the Church cannot remain disinterested in the problem during this waiting period.

First of all, there is a task for the Chinese Christians who live today in that immense country and who have not renounced their own faith. It is they who assure a presence of the Church in today's China. Before the revolution, this presence was made visible by the Catholic institutions such as schools, hospitals, research institutes, universities. These institutions were nationalized by the State. Christians can ensure the Church's presence only through the witness of their faith. "What is required from Christians today is the testimony of a personal existence renewed by faith. This faith geared to daily life, can only be nourished through common prayer and exchanges among fellow Christians in concrete life situations."[41] Their faith must be manifested "through a certain way of being in the world."[42]

We believe that Charbonnier and Trivière are right. Secularization in China is carried on in the most radical way. On every side it is repeated that God does not exist and that the true God of China is "the masses." Under these conditions, the proper circumstances are lacking for public evangelization. It must be limited to the right word exchanged at the right moment and especially to the testimony of one's life. This shows that faith gives existence a new dimension which reveals a perspective different from the one taught by Marxism in the schools and through the mass media. Materialism cannot satisfy people. The moment will come when they will note its shortcomings. This is precisely the right circumstance in which Christian life shows that there are other paths. Its task is to pose a problem in the hearts of those who believe they have found the definitive key for interpreting history. This will be the way to witness not only to the presence of Christianity in China but also to its special contribution to the construction of the earthly city which is so desired in that country.

Christian life which is intensely lived and witnessed will show the Chinese who live in the New China that humanity is not one-dimensional and that the moral values which Communism puts forth must also have a basis. A Christian way of existing and living will show how the Gospel is "the salt of the earth" and the "light of the world." This is what the first Christians did when persecution raged. They attested with their blood, when necessary, but especially with the example that their religion was "divine"—that, while being in the world, they pursued a destiny beyond the world.

Christians and the New China

The task of Christians in the universal Church is more urgent. They are or should be anxious to spread God's kingdom in the world, and they cannot leave China to its own destiny as if it did not concern them.

First of all, the entire Church and especially those mainly responsible for evangelization are obliged vis-à-vis the New China phenomenon to make an examination of conscience and ask themselves why the four attempts at evangelical penetration into that immense country have always ended in failure or were less successful than expected. This is a thought-provoking fact. Are Christians alone to blame, with their methods of evangelization and their attempt to import Western culture into China?

We do not feel that this question can be answered with an unqualified yes. We need to recall two important facts already mentioned: first, the great esteem which the Chinese have for their own culture and which makes it difficult for them to learn from others and, secondly, the very nature of Christianity which is not "according to human nature." Among the problems which Chinese intellectuals raised for Matteo Ricci, there was their constant difficulty in admitting that an event as important as the missionary believed Christianity to be had remained unknown to them and that this movement had arisen in the dim and distant West. It is the same question which the pagans of the Empire raised for the messengers of the Gospel and which received its classic response from Augustine.

Another no less important problem can be added which was also emphasized by some of the speakers at Båstad. So far Christianity has not only appeared to the Chinese as a religion from the "dim West" but also they saw in it, as others did, the aspect of "folly" which St. Paul speaks of with regard to Christ crucified (1 Corinthians 1, 23). Ricci himself, perhaps the most intelligent missionary to China, remained silent about this mystery in his first approach to Chinese culture and waited for the right moment to deal with it. Chinese culture, if you will excuse the expression, is too wise to accept easily a fact that is so minimally "wise" such as the incarnation, death and resurrection of the Word. Every nation and culture has its moment for arriving at faith. For this reason, Jesus wanted his Gospel to be propagated progressively in the world, in order to give the various nations time to become disposed to accept his message. Perhaps that moment had not yet arrived for China when the Church undertook its earlier attempts at evangelization. We have expressed the hope that Communism will aid this maturation process.

The Inculturation of Christianity

Communism has another merit which makes it the way prepared by God for announcing the Gospel in China when the opportune moment will arrive. It is that the Church will dispense with all those activities which gave it a Western aspect in China: schools, hospitals, universities, etc. The Church could not give up these institutions because they were her chosen means to show the Chinese people Christ's charity. However, in operating them, the missionaries could have mistakenly let them appear means of proselytism or even propaganda for Western culture. Furthermore, these works were supported with money from Christian countries and, at times, from the colonial powers who obviously were not disinterested in their "charity." Thus the missions with all their plants appeared or could have appeared in a false or repugnant light to the Chinese.

The New China, at least according to what is known, is giving itself a first-rate social and educational organization. This means that missionaries in the future, when they have the opportunity again to proclaim the Gospel in China, can do without these works. They will announce the divine plan of salvation to the Chinese, the love of God for humanity which is not a Western reality, and they will do it in a truly Chinese language and culture.

While the new Chinese society develops, a process is taking place in the West—the "de-Westernizing" of Christianity. It grew up in Asia in a Semitic culture, but became fully acclimatized in the classical culture. We do not know if this culture is especially appropriate for receiving and assimilating Christian values. Christianity, in fact, has profoundly affected the West and its culture to the point that today Western culture—and we do not argue that this is right or wrong—is still called "Christian culture." This, however, does not mean that Christianity remains so linked to this culture that it is identified with it and that it is impossible to Christianize without Westernizing. By now this identification is rejected by everyone and the Second Vatican Council has stated this most explicit.

With a view to taking up again its mission in China, the Church must study the ways and means for inserting the Gospel into the culture that is being formed in the New China. Hence comes the need, stressed by many speakers at Båstad and Louvain, to reform the language with which Christianity would be presented to the New China: a language which would keep in mind both the real content of the Christian message and the new situation created in China after 1949. It is a difficult and complicated task in which Chinese and Western Christians would have to collaborate. We know how much past missionaries worked even to find the precise expression for indicating God's name. From this we can understand what a delicate task awaits theologians.

All of this supposes a knowledge of Chinese culture and

sensibility which cannot be improvised. It is the fruit of long and patient research.

Christian Witness

Besides engaging in self-criticism and preparing to present a Christianity which will let the Chinese see what it really is without political and cultural deformations, what is mainly required of the Church is life witness. Before announcing the Gospel, the Church must show what the Gospel really means in the lives of people. This is its most important task without which the others risk losing their effectiveness.

In this connection, it is interesting to refer to a theme which we find in the Båstad lectures: the New China's "challenge" to Christianity.[44] After having spoken of the New China and the spirit which has developed there, Donald MacInnis cites Hosea Williams: "We therefore ask America: due to religious hypocrisy, is it possible that God has become so disgusted with the 'believers' that he has decided to turn the moral future of mankind over to non-believers? Is it possible that Christianity is too important to be left in the hands of today's so-called Christians. . . ?"[45] These are truly harsh words which mesh with those of an Anglican ex-missionary to China: "Our mandate has been withdrawn" and "the end of the missionary era was the will of God."[46] We cannot, however, accept these opinions because they are contrary to the Bible which is the word of God for us. The word of truth entrusted to the Church must, with Christ's help, resound to the ends of the earth (Acts 1,8) and until the end of the world (Matthew 28,16-20). No. Humanity's religious future remains entrusted to the Church no matter how imperfect its members may be. God did not turn to non-believers; he has not taken back the mandate conferred on the apostles and their successors, the college of Bishops united to the Pope. The missionary era is not over and will not be over so long as there are people to be evangelized including those living in the New China.

Nevertheless, Christians must seriously reflect the opinions expressed by Williams and others. They are dictated both by the observation of the Chinese reality which—at least according to reports—commands respect and admiration, and by the collapse of an evangelization to which the evil behavior by Christians was not foreign. The Church not only must avoid identifying itself with those nations which have exploited the poor of the Third World. It should also engage in an internal renewal, eliminating in itself everything which covers the face of Christ. In a secularized world, the Church must show what the Good News of salvation is and how it changes human life by giving it a new direction.

This point holds true for the whole task of the Church in a secularized world. To a world bent on creating an earthly city which totally leaves out God, the Church must show that this can be realized in a way favorable to people only through the love which is the essence of the Christian message. Both love of God and love of human beings are necessary. There is no reason to love people if we cannot see in them our own brothers and sisters who belong to the same family, to the same Father who has mysteriously generated us and made us his adopted sons and daughters. Only this perspective will make the earthly city which is being built with so much effort the city of people and not some monster which devours its own children by dehumanizing them. Now more than ever the Gospel's words have their value. Jesus called his followers the "light of the earth" and the "salt of the earth." Without light, things cannot be seen in their true nature and in the function they have for human life. And without salt they can have no taste nor be worthy of being taken seriously and lived.

Such is the contribution which all Christians can and must make to the world that is emerging. This is the witness which will allow the New China to see that the Gospel—far from being a product foreign to her culture—is what she needs in order that her political, social and economic victories be truly human. Thus China can create a new humanity that is new, not only with respect to the old, pre-1949 one, but because it is reborn to a new life, that of God's sons and daughters.

NOTES

1. "Love and Animosity in the Ethic of Mao," *Båstad*, p. 72.
2. *Ibid.*, p. 73.
3. *Ibid.*, p. 78.
4. *Ibid.*, p. 81.
5. *Ibid.*, p. 81.
6. *Ibid.*, p. 83.
7. Choang-seng Song, "The New China and Salvation History. A Methodological Enquiry," *Båstad*, p. 116.
8. *Ibid.*, p. 116f.
9. *Ibid.*, p. 119, 121.
10. *Ibid.*, p. 122.
11. *Ibid.*, p. 122.
12. *Ibid.*, p. 123.
13. *Ibid.*, p. 123.
14. *Ibid.*, p. 124.
15. *Ibid.*, pp. 124, 126.
16. *Ibid.*, p. 127.
17. *Ibid.*, pp. 127, 128.
18. *Ibid.*, p. 129.
19. *Ibid.*, p. 131.
20. *Ibid.*, p. 121.
21. For the concept of salvation, we are indebted to the article "Salvation" in Xávier Léon-Dufour (ed.), *Dictionary of Biblical Theology.*
22. *Aplogia*, pp. 15-17.
23. *Letter to Diognetus*, pp. 5-6.
24. E. Bloch, *Das Prinzip Hoffnung* (Frankfurt, 1959), p. 1381.
25. A. Schaaf, *Marx oder Sartre?* (Europa Verlag, 1964), p. 33.
26. A. Schaaf, *Ibid.*, p. 65.
27. Bloch, *op. cit.*, p. 1299.
28. Bloch, *Ibid.*, p. 1297.
29. Cf. F. Ormea, "Marxisti di fronte alla morte," in *Dialogo*, (Brescia, 1970), pp. 7-32.
30. Bloch, *op. cit.*, p. 1299.
31. "Some Reports on China by Fides News Service," *Louvain*, pp. 124-125.
32. Jean Charbonnier and Léon Trevière, "The New China and the History of Salvation," *Båstad*, pp. 87ff.
33. *Nostra Aetate*, n.1
34. *Louvain*, p. 123.
35. Vatican II, *Ad Gentes*, n. 7.
36. Raymond L. Whitehead, "Love and Animosity in the Ethic of Mao," *Båstad*, p. 73.
37. *Pro Mundi Vita*, "China and the Churches in the Making of One World," *Louvain*, p. 22.

38. Max Horkheimer, *La nostalgia del totalmente Altro* (Brescia, 1971).
39. *Båstad*, p. 118.
40. *Louvain*, p. 72.
41. *Båstad*, p. 106.
42. *Båstad*, p. 107.
43. Cf. *Louvain*, p. 107.
44. *Båstad*, p. 96.
45. *Båstad*, p. 138.
46. *Louvain*, p. 25.

Christ and China

GERALD O'COLLINS, S.J.

It has been conventional to describe theology as "faith seeking understanding." We might, however, care to shift from the private sphere of understanding to the public sphere of language and call theology "watching one's language in the presence of God." Either way Christian theology must show itself to be truly Christian. It should seek understanding in the light of Jesus Christ. It should watch its language in the presence of the God-man.

Using either version of theology, what might we say about the New China and the recent Chinese experience? What insights and reflections do faith in Christ suggest about the era and the nation on which Mao Tse-tung has put his stamp? Where can belief in the crucified and risen Jesus take its stand vis-à-vis contemporary China?

When asked to confront Christ and Mao's China, I have no short or easy answer to give. Let me single out two themes (suffering and the emulation of heroes), and then conclude by rapidly listing some major points of comparison and contrast which emerge when we bring together the two figures themselves, Jesus and Mao.

I

First of all, suffering. Over twenty years ago, Fr. Robert W. Greene's *Calvary in China* appeared.[1] In 1937 he had begun his missionary career in China. He was imprisoned after the Communist victory in 1949, put on trial in 1952, and then expelled from the country.

124

The book describes the destruction of his mission and his own sufferings—especially the drawn-out trial which reaches a climax in Holy Week. At many points the story matches the passion of Jesus himself. Former Christians and friends act with Judas-like treachery. Greene recalls an old non-Christian as replaying the role of Simon of Cyrene (p. 97). At the trial itself the judge parallels Pilate's contempt for truth. His Communist lies confront the simple Christian truth which Greene represents.

In fact, the whole book sends us back to the high and carefully prepared drama of Christ's passion. The gospel story respects our sense of timing. Both sides set themselves on a collision course and keep to it. In Mark, the Pharisees and Herodians may initiate joint plans to kill Jesus as early as chapter three, verse six. In John's version, Jesus himself wastes little time before visiting Jerusalem, cleansing the temple and issuing his provocative statement about "destroying" the sacred place (2:13ff.). Nevertheless, both Jesus and those who line up against him do not rush at once to the climax. Tension must first mount. The story pushes forward steadily to the highpoint of the trial and public execution.

Greene frames the account of his sufferings in China with a similar dramatic sense. The Red soldiers and Communist peasants do not surge forward in violent rage to beat the missionary and fling him out of their country. The story wears an air of measured deliberateness: a long imprisonment, a series of examinations late into the night, a public trial at Easter before a crowd of at least six thousand people and—finally—expulsion from China.

During the night's hearings, false titles are heaped on Greene—"spy," "reactionary," "imperialist devil," "guerrilla accomplice" etc. Like Jesus he stands alone—without any advocate or friends present. His hands are tied behind him. A soldier slaps him across the face for giving a forceful answer to the officer conducting the trial. The missionary is charged with spying for the imperialist American government. False witnesses testify that he sent the guerrilla forces a revolver with which members of the People's Government Army had been killed.

Greene reports his feeling as he heard the charge: "If only this ordeal were being undergone for some doctrine of my Faith! But the political business gave me no consolation and left me with the thought only of its uselessness" (p. 135). The reader's mind flicks easily to the Lucan version of the proceedings before Pilate.

> Then the whole company of them [sc. elders of the people, both chief priests and scribes] arose, and brought him before Pilate. And they began to accuse him, saying, "We found this man perverting our nation, and forbidding us to give tribute to Caesar, and saying that he himself is Christ a king" (23:1-2).

Greene's sufferings raise questions about the feelings of Jesus before Pilate. Did our Savior feel distress at being tried not for some teaching drawn from the Sermon on the Mount, but for false and useless accusations drawn from the political world?

Greene recognizes and pursues the parallel between his story and the Lord's passion through detail after detail. He is kept short of water, but offers this unsatisfied thirst "to Our Lord for my persecuted Christians" (p. 131). By the end almost everyone seems to have turned on the missionary or left him. At the public trial his former cook acts as the star witness for the prosecution. Greene draws comfort from some Christian women whom he notices weeping over his torment. Finally, the crowd calls for the death penalty, "Kill him, kill him" (p. 148).

All in all, Greene's book skillfully and movingly describes his own way of the cross and the tragic destruction of a Christian community. It would be grossly unfair to belittle either the deep commitment or the very real pain of such veteran missionaries. I have dwelt on *Calvary in China* because of its implications for any theology of the cross in a Chinese context.

This book and similar works narrow down the possibilities for seeing links between (1) suffering in China and (2) the passion and crucifixion of Jesus. Greene invites us to grieve most of all over the sufferings of the Christian laypeople, sisters and priests. He also recounts the horrifying scenes he frequently witnessed: the dozens of public trials and executions which contributed to the ruthless political re-education of the people. Very occasionally he allows us to glimpse the wider sufferings that China endured for a century and more. Thus he speaks of his Communist persecutors:

> I was not in their eyes a simple Catholic priest who was trying quietly to preach the doctrine of Christ among them. I was a symbol of something they hated long before Communism raised its ugly head in their land. It was the West they saw in me. The West that had for years humiliated and degraded China—and in my heart I knew these crimes of the Christian West cried for change (p. 129).

As a total work, however, *Calvary in China* entails its special risks. With other such books from the forties and fifties it seduced readers into concentrating on the sufferings of individual Christians—often notable and brave leaders—and into disregarding the way of the cross walked by anonymous millions in Asia, Europe and elsewhere.

Take China itself. During the Sino-Japanese war (1937-45) well over twenty million Chinese died. Wars, bandits, famines and floods destroyed at least forty million Chinese in the first half of this century. In a thousand ways, human beings and nature proved themselves prone to seek out and destroy Chinese men and women. The perspective of killing permeated the history of China for decades before Mao came to power. Of course, these victims have remained, for the most part, an anonymous mass for the "Christian" West: soldiers rushing to death on some distant Chinese battlefield, civilians left dead after a Japanese bombing raid, all the casualties of the cruel civil war, the landlords and capitalists purged after the People's Republic came into being. The word "Calvary" can take on new overtones when we recall those large crowds of Chinese whose butchery we can only mourn *en masse*.

God forbid that missionaries like Greene bear the blame for the extraordinary way Western Christians have permitted themselves to ignore and blank out the enormous suffering endured by the Chinese and other non-Christians. Significantly, "Hiroshima" is one of the few names from Asia which continues to symbolize man's relentless inhumanity to man. Would this have been so, if by 1945 the Japanese had not already proved themselves fit candidates for the Western club of capitalists?

Let us also not pass over the fact that the martyrdom of Jesus has stamped the imagination of the West. Men stalked and killed Jesus. His death left behind its very particular scar on human memory. After his name those of such martyrs as Joan of Arc, Thomas More and Dietrich Bonhoeffer glitter like gold. They refused to step out in the darkness of cowardly capitulation. Their courage transmuted death into a precious event, the end which gave point and purpose to their whole existence. The execution of Jesus himself and of the martyrs who imitated his heroism has impressed itself sharply on the Western mind. Could it be that Christians have become so oriented toward the model of the individual martyr that they are a little more ready to shrug off the atrocious slaughter of millions of their brothers and sisters?

Here I cannot help wondering whether books like *Calvary in China*—against the intentions of their authors—contributed to the widespread and ruthless indifference toward the dead of Biafra, Chile, Iraq, Vietnam, and all those other scenes of mass death. Where a book or a film clearly frames the sufferings of some noble individual, we open ourselves to feel anger or pain. But anonymous, large-scale deaths can leave us unmoved. A Calvary in China is only for individual Christian heroes and heroines.

In one major way books like *Calvary in China* "improved on" the passion story and—notoriously—helped to anaesthetize Western consciences toward countries that either turned Communist or needed to be rescued from Communism at all costs. Opposition to "diabolic Communism" could be pressed into service to excuse countless acts of savagery.

Greene begins with the familiar comparison between Communism and Catholicism. Communism resembles the Catholic Church by its insistence on unity, universality and apostolicity, as well as by such practices as the confession of faults. After that comparison it then becomes easier to slip into talking about a mortal combat between the Cross and the Hammer and Sickle. Greene can press on to recall the satanic sense communicated by the officials before whom he appeared. He was accused of calling Communist officials "devils." A "smug and sinister" smile lit up the face of the judge when he heard that word, "devils" (p. 142).

This sense of confrontation with personified evil fails, however, to show up in the case of Jesus' trial and death. In Mark's gospel, Jesus shows himself from the outset of the ministry clearly "the stronger man" (3:27)—driving out demons and effortlessly overcoming the invisible powers of evil. But once the passion and crucifixion begin to loom up, the exorcisms drop away. Apart from the isolated case of one possessed boy (9:14-29), we never hear of any evil spirits again. In Luke's passion story, Satan enters into Judas (22:3), Peter is warned that Satan wishes to "sift him like wheat" (22:31), and Jesus surrenders to those who arrest him: "This is your hour, and the power of darkness" (22:53). But any sense that Jesus goes to battle against demonic powers peters out at that point. John's gospel names Satan as "a murderer from the beginning," who "has nothing to do with truth" (8:44) and who enters into Judas at the last supper (13:27). Yet this "entrance" is also Satan's exit from the story.

In fact, the trial and crucifixion narratives do not yield any sense of confrontation with Satan's representatives. Take Mark's story, for instance. At the night trial the high priest meets Jesus for the first and only time. We are not told that Caiaphas' face comes to life with a diabolic smile when he finally sees the prisoner. Mark neither adds any such sinister details nor—for that matter—even gives the high priest's name. He simply drops him into the narrative for a brief burst of questioning. Caiaphas quickly reaches his key demand, "Are you the Christ, the Son of the Blessed?" Once he hears the affirmative answer, he turns from the prisoner to ask other members of the council: "Why do we still need witnesses? You have heard his blasphemy. What is your decision?" (14:60-64). He neither shows demonic rage at the claim nor makes any attempt to get Jesus to disown the claim.

Neither Caiaphas nor Pilate have wickedly schemed to pervert the world. They simply act to protect their power, property and privileges. A certain moral indifference allows them to defend their "interests," even though that means killing an innocent and vulnerable man. From the little we see of Pilate and the priests in the gospel story—or can learn of them from elsewhere—they do not look like totally monstrous persons who have entered into some league with the devil and the invisible powers of evil. Pilate and Caiaphas have value-systems that seem coherent, intelligible and even uncomfortably like our own. Call them ruthless and morally indifferent, but *not* frontmen for Satan himself.

Of course, the situation in modern China, unlike that of the ancient Roman Empire, makes it easier for Greene to suggest forces and figures that loom larger than the ordinary life of man. As supreme hero and universal savior of China, Mao makes himself constantly present. Communism offers a consistent and compulsory explanation of life in all its aspects. Neither Pilate nor Caiaphas nor even Tiberius Caesar matches Mao. None of them have his stature, demonic or otherwise. Despite official emperor worship, the Roman rule allowed for a generous diversity of religious (and agnostic) beliefs and practices. Imperial Rome did not expect or impose a single, all-encompassing world-view, as happens in Mao's China. It is more plausible for Greene than it was for the evangelists to hint at invisible agents of evil. More readily than the passion narratives, *Calvary in China* can encourage its readers to look beyond a particular set of human beings to the unseen powers of darkness.

Undoubtedly, Greene has some New Testament warrant for making such a move when telling the story of his suffering. The letter to the Ephesians describes Christian life in the following terms:

> Put on the whole armor of God, that you may be able to stand against the wiles of the devil. For we are not contend-

ing against flesh and blood, but against the principalities, against the powers, against the world rulers of this present darkness, against the spiritual hosts of wickedness in the heavenly places. Therefore take the whole armor of God, that you may be able to withstand in the evil day, and having done all, to stand (6:11-13).

Nevertheless, it is worth reminding ourselves here of two points. First, the Gospels portray Jesus as sweeping before him the unseen powers of evil. Unhesitatingly, he sees through the diabolic temptations that confront him in the desert. There is never any doubt that he might fail in standing up to the invisible forces of Satan. No New Testament writer speaks of Jesus needing to "put on the whole armor of God, that he might be able to stand against the wiles of the devil." Second, in II Corinthians St. Paul repeatedly recalls the sufferings he went through as a result of preaching the Good News. His meditation on Christ's passion merges with a meditation on his own suffering mission.

Five times I have received at the hands of the Jews the forty lashes less one. Three times I have been beaten with rods; once I was stoned. Three times I have been shipwrecked; a night and a day I have been adrift at sea; on frequent journeys, in danger from rivers, danger from robbers, danger from my own people, danger from Gentiles, danger in the city, danger in the wilderness, danger at sea, danger from false brethren; in toil and hardship, through many a sleepless night, in hunger and thirst, often without food, in cold and exposure (11:24-27).

Paul feels drawn into the event of the crucifixion. But he does not represent his participation in the Lord's passion as conflict with demonic powers. Thoroughly visible agents (Jews, Gentiles, robbers, etc.) and forces of nature (the sea, flooded rivers, cold, etc.) strike at and threaten to kill Paul.

A few words of summary are in order. I shrink from my remarks about Fr. Greene's book being taken as another dreary example of heartless disregard for heroic missionaries. Criticism looks cheap coming from well-fed academics sitting in their offices twenty years later. Nevertheless, I find at least two deeply disturbing implications in *Calvary in China.*

Firstly, it pushes the understanding of Christian suffering beyond the plane of harsh secular realities to a mythical level. There Chinese and other Communists begin to look like the puppets and mouthpieces of Satan. Thomas Berry's paper ("Mao Tse-tung: The Long March. A Study in Revolutionary Antagonism and Christian Love") tugs at our elbow, and says that it is nonsense to view Mao as some satanic anti-Christ. It seems much more reasonable to argue that Mao has been locked in a struggle with another invisible figure—Confucius.

> The key to understanding Mao is in recognizing in him a counter-Confucius, whose greatest historical mission, in spite of himself, is to evoke a renewal of the Confucian tradition. Confucius will one day be recognized as the colossus of Chinese tradition who challenged Mao as consistently as Mao challenged him. Confucius can even now be seen as the hidden anxiety of Mao, as the judge of his deeds, the one against whom Mao was struggling throughout the entire course of the Cultural Revolution, and the one whom Mao had in mind everytime he mentioned the word 'struggle.' Until this day, Confucius remains both the inspiration and the indestructible nemesis of Mao.[2]

In short, Mao is a counter-Confucius, not a counter-Christ.

Second, books like *Calvary in China* have encouraged their readers to relate Christ's passion *only to Christian suffering.* Any proper theology of the cross, however, dares not evade the enormous mass of suffering undergone by the Chinese people at large. Even before theologians begin to reflect on the *gesta Dei per Sinenses* (the acts of God through the Chinese), they need to recognize the full extent of the *passio Christi apud Sinenses* (the passion of Christ among the Chinese).

In his "Love and Animosity in the Ethic of Mao," Raymond Whitehead spots Reinhold Niebuhr's tendency to relate Calvary only to that loving suffering of individuals which Christianity has honored. Niebuhr wrote in his *Moral Man and Immoral Society:*

> Meanwhile it must be admitted that no society will ever be so just, that some method of escape from its cruelties will not be sought by the pure heart. The devotion of Christianity to the cross is an unconscious glorification of *the individual moral ideal.* The cross is the symbol of love triumphant in its own integrity, but not triumphant in the world and society.[3]

Whitehead refuses to separate in this fashion "the individual moral ideal from *social struggle.* We live not simply as individuals but in social contexts, in classes. The cross must be related to *class struggle.*"[4] Nevertheless, even Whitehead pushes aside the full implications of Calvary. Any adequate theology of the cross must remember not only the classes actively locked in social struggle, but also all those classes and individuals who are or have been the passive victims of conflict.

The *passio Christi apud Sinenses* must be taken in its full range. Calvary in China covers not only the heroic dead of the Communist Liberation Army, but also the victims of Nanking, Kuomintang casualties, prisoners in labor camps, and all those professionals and academics who have seen their disciplines suppressed after the Communist Revolution. Let us reflect for a moment on this last group. Rejected as bourgeois, anthropologists, psychologists and sociologists can live only by finding a substitute job. They saw their chosen work ending in bitter failure. There is at least some faint analogy here to the failure Jesus himself experienced. After accepting his vocation to renew the spiritual life of Israel, he soon found almost everyone standing against him. He could only weep over Jerusalem, the city he wished to convert (Luke 19:41).

In brief, faith seeking an understanding of China must take the full scope of Chinese suffering into account. Pascal remarked that "Jesus will be in agony to the end of the world." That agony includes the whole way of the cross along which the Chinese people have passed and continue to pass.

Several of the papers at the Båstad seminar and the Louvain colloquium invite the comment, "Your Calvary is not big enough." Jean Charbonnier and Léon Trivière (on "The New China and the History of Salvation") seem to do better. "Sufferings," they write, "endured by millions of Chinese in the work of shaping their nation into a new people give them a share in the redemptive passion of the Savior."[5] Heaven forbid that I should allow niggling criticism or scoring off other writers to look like the first objective of my essay. But I suspect that Charbonnier and Trivière suggest all too readily only the conscious acceptance of suffering by Chinese who hoped to shape "their nation into a new people." But Christ's cross casts its shadow over all the victims of man's vicious inhumanity to man: children butchered by mad tyrants, Jews herded to their death in shower-rooms, and Chinese lives cut short by warlords, Japanese invaders and natural disasters, as well as the lives freely given to bring about the New China.

II

Closely aligned with the theme of the *passio Christi apud Sinenses* is that of the emulation of heroes. Mao has led his nation in an extraordinary struggle to reshape the values, attitudes and ideas of an entire people. James Reston, senior editor of the *New York Times* was astounded by "the staggering thing that modern China is trying to do. They're not trying merely to revolutionize people, and establish a sense of social conscience, but they're really trying to change the character of these people. The place is one vast school of moral philosophy."[6] Many methods pour into this enormous programme of thought-reform: preaching, teaching, wide-ranging techniques of persuasion from the outside, and orgies of self-criticism in which people testify to their conversion away from selfishness and incorrect ideas toward an exalted service of the masses in the name of the party. In all this ideological struggle to practice good deeds, overcome selfishness and reach true equality in a new society—the emulation of heroes (and sometimes of heroines) has emerged as a major means used on a nation-wide scale.

I would like to explore this imitation of heroes. It would be silly to speak of it constituting an *imitatio Christi apud Sinenses* (imitation of Christ among the Chinese). Nevertheless, certain interesting Christological implications may emerge.

Both the theater and literature hold up figures for popular imitation in China. Traditional theatrical forms have disappeared. The New Chinese theater pays honor to war heroes, members of the Long March, and other martyrs who gave their lives for Chairman Mao and the people. *The Red Lantern* celebrates a proletarian hero, Li Yu-ho. A Japanese squad shoots this railway pointsman. In *The Red Detachment of Woman* Hong Chang-ching dies on a pyre, a burnt victim in the cause of revolution.

Booklets like *Fear neither Hardship nor Death in Serving the People, A Worthy Son of the People* and *A Brave Fighter for Communism* retail heroic stories of young soldiers and other folk heroes. The Tachai production brigade became an example to the whole nation, when they effectively overcame massive agricultural problems. The 1970 *Peking Review* eulogizes Comrade Hsün-hua for dying "a martyr's death." This young intellectual had volunteered for manual labor in Manchuria. He lost his life trying to save some poles swept away by a flooded river.

Mao himself, of course, towers over all the figures proposed for admiration and imitation. Klaus Mehnert sums up the position this way:

> Never has a man been so undevotedly, uncritically and enthusiastically honored during his lifetime as Chairman Mao is today. . . . The Mao cult is one of the greatest triumphs of publicity in a publicity-conscious age.[7]

Is there any Christological significance to uncover in all this Chinese praise of "famous men, the heroes of their nation's history" (Wisdom 44:1)? Take the encomium which Mao Tsetung delivered to commemorate a common soldier, Chang Szu-teh, who had died when a kiln collapsed while he was making charcoal for the people:

> All men must die, but death can vary in its significance. The ancient Chinese writer Szuma Chien said, "Though death befalls all men alike, it may be weightier than Mount Tai or lighter than a feather." To die for the people is weightier than Mount Tai, but to work for the fascists and die for the exploiters and oppressors is lighter than a feather. Comrade Chang Szu-teh died for the people, and his death is indeed weightier than Mount Tai.[8]

An article by Mary Sheridan "The Emulation of Heroes" can point us in the right direction. Imitating heroes, she reminds us, is scarcely a Communist invention. "It was a mainstay of Confucian education in the form of stories about great emperors, generals, poets, magistrates, and filial children." And—one might add—emulation of heroes has pervaded other cultures and periods, not least Christianity itself which has normally kept popularizing hagiographers fully employed. But what sets the Communist system apart, Sheridan remarks, is

> (1) the careful ideological control of the hero characterisations, action and language by which the ideological "message" is conveyed; (2) the use of nation-wide campaigns so that all children (and adults) are emulating the *same* hero at the same time; (3) the degree of intensity and active participation encouraged (p. 47).

What may turn out to be helpful for our reflections here are the heroes chosen rather than the campaigns used to popularize them. Let me take up some examples of the figures that have received China-wide publicity.

Apart from the great leaders of the Communist Party, most of the heroes and martyrs who have been proposed as models come from the lowest ranks: heroic soldiers who fell in the civil war or the Korean war, martyrs of the Japanese invasion, heroic workers from the days when the Communists were confined to Yenan. Among those held up as models for imitation some died sacrificing their lives in accidents. Ouyang Hai pushed a horse loaded with ammunition out of the path of an oncoming train. Wang Chieh threw himself on a defective mine to save the lives of the soldiers he was instructing. Liu Ying-chün died rescuing some children from runaway horses.

The last two heroes left diaries behind. In both cases one notices, peeping over their shoulders, the looming figures of Chairman Mao and the Party. The diaries quote Mao, refer to him often and mention the Party frequently. Wang Chieh records some of his good deeds. Liu Ying-chün appears thoroughly intent on examining his mistakes, cultivating the revolutionary spirit and establishing correct patterns of thought. They become heroes by applying Mao's thought each day. After death their attitude toward life is found mirrored in their diaries. There the motivation for their ultimate self-sacrifice appears. As Sheridan observes,

this point is important to the Maoists that they take every care in the diaries to avoid the accusation that a hero's death might be the result of a "momentary righteous impulse." It is the exemplary life and specifically the Maoist education, which alone makes possible the noble death (p. 57).

Do such modern Chinese heroes relate in any way to the crucified figure on Calvary? Many of them resemble Jesus in dying young—in fact often in their early twenties. The moral effect of their lives and deaths encourages others to endorse Mao's thought and the Communist Revolution—even to the point of being ready to lose their lives in that cause. The majority of these models of virtue are—like Jesus—male rather than female.

Beyond question, some formal comparisons call for our attention. But we cannot move more than a step or two from this common ground without stumbling over major differences. First, none of these examples of Communist virtue is truly credited with universal and lasting significance. The story of one heroic life follows the story of another heroic life. Even if nation-wide campaigns do ensure that "*all* children (and adults) are emulating the same hero at the same time," no single hero proves to be absolutely satisfying. Somehow his impact remains restricted. If Wang Chieh and others establish a pattern of new persons fashioned by Mao's vision, they are no more than the first representatives of a quick succession of heroes. In effect, no claim is made that any hero's death offers a *uniquely* precious appeal for conversion and self-dedication.

Second, the Communist heroes may die, but success attends their self-sacrifice. The train was saved. The defective mine causes only the death of Wang Chieh. The runaway horses and their wagon do not kill the group of children. The execution on Calvary, however, does not *seem* to save anyone. To all appearances, that death rescues no one from any danger or evil. The crucifixion can look like an extreme case among pointless atrocities, a disturbing example of meaningless disorder which achieves nothing.

Third, the kind of deaths which the revolutionary heroes of China die seemingly bears little resemblance to Calvary. Take the end of Hai Ouyang. He saves a train, but is fatally crushed beneath its wheels and dies in a hospital.

> Hai lay quietly on his bed, the blood of class brothers flowing into his body, slowly, drop by drop, through a transfusion tube. He was so calm, so peaceful. On his face there was no trace of pain. It was as if he had just returned from completing some task and was smilingly thinking of taking up another and heavier load for socialist construction. His deep, clear eyes seemed to glow, and several times he moved his lips, trying to speak. He smiled as if he had already discovered the secret of the defense plant.
>
> Suddenly the flow of blood through the tube ceased. Hai's heart had stopped beating. His eyes slowly closed. A short and glorious life of twenty-three years had come to an end.
>
> On the hill-tops of Phoenix Village the sun was shining. The pine tree at the Ouyang family door, washed clean

by the recent rain, looked especially straight and green. Many pine nuts had sprouted at its foot and healthy saplings were growing in the sunlight.

The pine tree stood like a hero's monument erected on the hill-top, erected in the people's hearts, eternal, for all generations to come.[10]

As Mary Sheridan comments, for such a hero "death holds neither pain, nor fear, nor disfigurement. Transfixed by inner visions, the hero watches himself pass into immortality. He dies in spiritual certainty" (p. 61). All of this may be moving and romantic, but the style of death has little to do with the squalid sadism of Calvary. When he died by that vicious combination of impalement and display practiced by the Romans, Jesus cried out: "My God, my God, why hast thou forsaken me?"

One can go on piling up the contrasts between the execution on Calvary and the self-sacrifice of Communist heroes. Their deaths fail to resemble, let alone match, the death of Jesus—either at the visible level or at the level of what is believed to have taken place. Does all that rule out any valuable link between the heroes proposed for emulation in the New China and Jesus, the ultimate hero for Christian faith? Can we advance beyond the general point that in both cases we deal with moral examples, men who gave their lives for others in a spirit of loving disregard of self-interest?

Mary Sheridan suggests a comparison which offers a way in. On the one hand, "the classical heroes were admired by their contemporaries for their real superiority in natural endowments. Achilles was such a hero 'by nature'." On the other hand, "none of the new Chinese heroes have superior natural endowments." Wang Chieh, for instance, "is anything but well endowed" (p. 56).

This brings to mind St. Paul's reflections on Christ's fate and on Christian participation in the crucifixion as revealing *power in weakness*. Looking only at the natural qualifications of the Chinese figures held up for emulation, we might not expect any heroic performance or self-sacrifice. Yet power comes to these heroes and martyrs, despite their limited capacities.

Quite ordinary soldiers from the People's Liberation Army prove capable not only of hard work but of utterly selfless patriotism. They become heroic and powerful. The strength to save others (like comrades or children) bursts through their weakness. Power comes to these Chinese heroes, because they have reflected on Mao's thought. Simply hearing the words of Chairman Mao can produce powerful effects. At the point of drowning in icy water, one Red Guard "heard the shouting on the shores: 'Be resolute, do not fear sacrifice, overcome every difficulty, be victorious.' Suddenly he acquired new energy."[11]

In brief, the Communist heroes and martyrs exemplify *in their own way* the Pauline principle of power in weakness. The source of their strength is not, of course, the death and resurrection of Christ, but the thought of Chairman Mao. What emerges if we confront the figures of Jesus and Mao? Let us turn to that in the concluding section of this essay.

III

If this piece on "Christ and China" is not to remain patently incomplete, the relationship between Christ and Mao needs to be tackled. And yet such a theme may leave us feeling like blind men standing around an elephant. They can size it up, but they cannot really take it in.

We can check off easily enough a number of formal contrasts. First, even if Mao's thought sometimes appears to be credited with miraculous results, no one attributes truly divine characteristics to him. Communist belief stops an extremely long way short of viewing him as the Word become flesh who dwelt among us to share his divine glory with us. Second, Jesus never published even a scrap of papyrus, let alone any series of works. In no sense did his influence spread by means of what he himself wrote. In the case of Chairman Mao, Mehnert can quite confidently assert that "never before in history have the writings of a single individual been published in such quantities."[12] When Mehnert wrote his book in the early 1970s, over seven hundred million copies of the *Little Red Book* were in print. There was a copy for every person in China.

Third, the teaching offered by Mao fails to match in essential ways the Gospel of Jesus. Three words, "self-help," "violence" and "utopia" gather together some of the major differences. The *Little Red Book* calls for "regeneration through our own efforts" (p. 194). Mao encourages the will to rise through one's own determination. He comes down on the side of human freedom rather than that of any iron laws of history. Aided by correct education, the decisive efforts of individuals will perfect human existence. Donald MacInnis puts the point this way:

> The Maoist modification of Marxist theory lays greater stress on man's capacity for inner-directed change in response to mental stimuli, rather than response only to social, economic and natural forces. Mao believes that conversion to new values can be hastened, that man's value changes are not tied to a rigid historical determinism.[13]

Do-it-yourself Maoism finds its classic expression in the parable of the Foolish Old Man Who Removed the Mountains. The lesson is clear. The aggressive will of the people triumphs rather than any blind forces of nature and history or any supernatural help from heaven. All of this stress on self-help takes us a long way from Jesus' call to *accept* the kingdom. If his invitation to repent and believe in the Good News affirmed the human freedom to say "yes" or "no" in the face of divine grace, he was not proclaiming a do-it-yourself salvation.

The best known sentence from the *Little Red Book* announces that "political power grows out of the barrel of a gun" (p. 61). Ninian Smart has recently argued that Mao's greatest achievement lies in his shaping a new spiritual force. Power grows out of the barrel of the spirit.[14] It may well be so. Nevertheless, granted that Mao has never shown himself a paranoid killer like Stalin, he views opponents as people to be ruthlessly crushed or forcibly re-educated. Violent class struggles shape his vision. He dismisses love of the oppressors for the oppressed as paternalism, and love of the oppressed for their oppressors as servility. Mao's implicit rejection of that Christian love which transcends class conflict and hostility has been quoted a thousand times. But one more time won't hurt.

> There will be a genuine love of humanity after classes are eliminated all over the world. Classes have split society into many antagonistic groupings; there will be love of all humanity when classes are eliminated, but not now. We cannot love enemies, we cannot love social evils, our aim is to destroy them.[15]

Jesus, however, preached love for one's enemies. He did not join the Zealot guerrilla forces. In fact he was so uninterested in combating imperialism, that his preaching hardly indicates that he lived in an occupied country under the Roman Empire.

Finally, it has become conventional to remark that the Marxist utopia represents a secularized version of God's kingdom. Mao has turned China into "one vast school of moral philosophy," because he hopes that the revolutionary struggle will in the end bring a good life for everyone. For its part, the Christian Gospel joyfully expects the consummation when God comes to be all things to everyone.

We have lined up some major contrasts between (1) Maoism and (2) the Christian faith, which bases itself on the life, death and resurrection of Jesus. We can also sort out some points of convergence. To begin with, Mao has effectively worked against the subjugation of women. He has destroyed concubinage, given women equal opportunities, and made Chinese women the envy of their sisters in the Western countries. There women still seem condemned in many ways to be little more than objects. Jesus, for his part, announced a new brotherhood and sisterhood based on doing the will of God: "Whoever does the will of God is my brother, my sister, my mother" (Mark 3:35). St. Paul proclaimed a revolutionary equality of men and women 'in Christ Jesus' (Galatians 3:28). This new life abolished any superiority and inferiority based on sexual difference. The later Christian Church tried in some ways to rescue women from pre-Christian indignities inflicted on them. When Christianity reached East Asia, it did help the position of women there. Nevertheless, both in China and elsewhere the organization of the Catholic Church has clearly asserted a privileged and preferential position for men. It was Mao's rule rather than the Christian missions which allowed women in China to make a huge leap forward in their rights and responsibilities. As Julia Ching observes, "Women are present in the Chinese Communist Party's Central Committee, but not in the College of Cardinals."[16]

Second, Mao "finds truth in the dialectical relationship of idea and practice."[17] True knowledge results from activity and experience—from the shared enterprise of living and studying the Marxist way of life. In his turn Jesus did not offer a system of truths to be understood but called people to discipleship. His truth was not merely an object of intellectual reflection, but a way of life to be followed. Both for Mao and Jesus issues of truth cannot be settled by theoretical deliberation alone.

Third, from the 1920s Mao drew attention to religion as one of the oppressive elements in Chinese society. An examination of the state of the Hunanese peasants led him to identify religious authority (along with political and clan authority) as one of the three systems which dominated the Chinese. It would, of course, be monstrously absurd to represent Jesus as opposed to religion and religious authority as such. Nevertheless, he realized how crushing the misuse of religious authority could be. He kept his harshest words for those leaders who oppressed the people by their misguided but authoritative interpretations of God's law.

Fourth, Jesus came preaching the presence of God's kingdom—that unique peak of salvation history which offers men opportunities which must be accepted now or lost forever. Mao's essay *On Practice* reflects a somewhat similar sense that human history has reached an unprecedented peak. He speaks of "the moment for completely banishing darkness from the world and from China and for changing the world into a world of light such as never previously existed."

I am putting aside scruples here and pulling in themes almost at random. They can serve to illustrate convergences and parallels between the teaching of Mao and the Good News brought by Jesus Christ. Julia Ching rightly warns against being content with any "simple avowal of Christian values in Mao's teachings."[18] Where then does the confrontation of Chairman Mao and Jesus leave us? Is there any one major point that we might draw from our attempt to list the likenesses and the differences?

All in all, no one should deny the enormous contrast which exists—between both the persons of Jesus and Mao and their doctrines. Take the external aspect of their lives. Born in 1893, Mao survived imprisonment, the Long March, the Sino-Japanese war and all the stages of the civil war to stand before a huge crowd in Peking and proclaim the foundation of the People's Republic in 1949. He lives today—this idolized leader of eight hundred million people. Jesus, however, did not pass through such a long life of intense activity. At most his ministry lasted three years. During that time he enjoyed some popularity with a few thousand people, but nothing like the obsessive admiration from the most numerous nation the world has ever seen.

Yet we may wonder how long the vast personality cult of Mao will last, once he departs the scene. Has he only a precarious grip on the imagination of the Chinese and humankind? If Jesus' appeal during life remained limited to sections of the Palestinian population and proved insufficient to save him from public execution, his appeal after death has spread throughout the world and shows no sign of decreasing after two thousand years. Quite apart from claims about his ontological status as Son of God and Savior of humanity, the very external features of his life, impact and teaching falsify any efforts to align Jesus and Mao too closely.

To conclude. This paper has tried to take to heart Julia Ching's suggestion about doing "Christian theology in a Chinese context."[19] Call it, if you will, "watching one's Christian language in the presence of China." If the attempt has contributed just a little to the quest for the right language about Jesus Christ in the second half of the twentieth century—the era of Mao Tse-tung—I will be grateful.

NOTES

1. London, 1954.
2. *Båstad*, p. 68.
3. (New York, 1932), pp. 81f.; italics mine.
4. *Båstad*, p. 82; italics mine.
5. *Båstad*, p. 108.
6. *New York Times*, September 1, 1971.
7. *China Today* (London, 1972), p. 209.
8. Mao Tse-tung, *Selected Works of Mao Tse-tung* (Peking, 1967), III, pp. 177f.
9. *China Quarterly* 33-36 (1968), pp. 47-72.
10. *Chinese Literature*, November 1966, pp. 103-04; cited Mary Sheridan, *op. cit.*, p. 61.
11. Cited Sheridan, *op. cit.*, p. 70.
12. *China Today*, p. 255.
13. *Båstad*, p. 148.
14. *Mao* (London, 1974).
15. *Selected Works of Mao Tse-tung*, III, pp. 90f.
16. *Båstad*, p. 31.
17. W. Glüer, *Båstad*, p. 50.
18. *Båstad*, p. 29.
19. "The Christian Way and the Chinese Wall," *America*, November 9, 1974, p. 278.

Theological Implications of the "New China"

FRANCIS A. SULLIVAN, S.J.

Many of the participants in the Bastad-Louvain colloquia have seen in the emergence of the "New China" a working out of God's plan of salvation for the Chinese people. In R. Whitehead's opinion, this has been a "reality of salvation outside the Church"[1] which he would number among "the most important events of salvation history in the mid-20th century."[2] Charbonnier and Trivière call upon Christians to recognize "promising signs of salvation" in the "Chinese way to the development of man."[3] C. S. Song's thesis is that "what we have in New China is a secularized version of salvation history."[4] R. Madsen argues that "it is possible to see in the experience of the men who have re-made China an experience of God's gift of salvation."[5]

I believe it would be helpful to distinguish three premises involved in reaching such a judgment about what has happened in China. As I see it, the premises are: 1) the acceptance as true, of the favorable reports which many recent visitors to the People's Republic of China have brought back to the Western world; 2) the acceptance of what one may call a "secularized" concept of salvation; and 3) the recognition of signs of such salvation in the emergence of the "new humanity" and "new society" in China.

In the first part of this paper I intend to offer some reflections on each of these three premises, and on the conclusion that has been based on them. In the second part I shall consider the consequences which such a conclusion would have for our understanding of the Church as the "universal sacrament of salvation."

146

I

First Premise: Reliability of the Reports

The Christian observers who have concluded that the emergence of the "New China" has been an event of salvation for the Chinese, have been convinced of the reliability of the many favorable reports that have been coming out of China in the past few years, not only with regard to the remarkable progress made toward satisfying the material needs of this vast population, but more especially with regard to the moral progress made toward the development of a "new humanity" and "new society" in China. I do not mean to imply that these observers are unaware of the darker side of the picture, or that their impressions are unqualifiedly enthusiastic. But their judgment is clearly that typified by the following statement of *Pro Mundi Vita:* "A judgment that the New China has been *on the whole good for the people,* at least to an extent that constitutes a challenge to Western or Christian self-righteousness, could now claim to be based on the testimony of almost all recent visitors and of most recent scholarship."[6] At the same time, the *Pro Mundi Vita* report continues with a word of caution: "This is not to say that only the ignorant and the envious could now be cautious about accepting even that much. Given the admittedly closed and manipulative character of the society, the grounds for purely scholarly scepticism remain extraordinary. If few generalizations about life in the People's Republic remain uncontroverted, it is only partly because few fail to arouse strong subjective reactions among scholars themselves. It is also because, by the standards of historical verification applied elsewhere, few possible ones are in fact incontrovertible."[7]

Julia Ching has also described our present knowledge and information concerning China as "inadequate." Despite this reservation, she has not hesitated to speak of "China's apparent success in inspiring social equality and moral asceticism both within and without her own frontiers."[8] While admitting that there are "bad" features in China's revolutionary history, R. Madsen insists that "many Christians who have recently come to study the New China seem to agree that the good predominates heavily over the bad."[9] Indeed, Madsen lauds the "holy asceticism of the men who continue to make the revolution,"[10] asserting that "in the course of a revolutionary experience Chinese have been re-made into men who live not for themselves but for others to the point that they can face even death with a spirit of hope."[11]

For another contributor to the Louvain colloquium, however, the "new humanity" which many Western observers believe they have found in Mao's China is more a myth than a reality. A Chinese Christian who left China in the early 1970's, having lived in the People's Republic since its establishment, has this to say: "In recent years, some Western scholars have tended to describe people in Communist China as a kind of "New Man," with newly acquired qualities of devoted service and self-sacrifice, faithfully following Chairman Mao's moral exhortations in pursuit of lofty social goals. *This, however, is mainly the view of deluded observers from outside.*"[12] While agreeing that "the achievements of the Communist regime are impressive," and that "Mao's teachings, through pervasive indoctrination, have influenced to varying degrees the minds of the people," he nevertheless insists that "Maoist thought reform has hardly touched the soul of the people, or brought a true conversion and rebirth in the image of the Maoist selfless man, which the Chairman himself is not."[13] Another Chinese contributor to the colloquia, P. Shen, also raises serious doubts about the picture of the "New China" that many Western observers have formed. As he puts it: "The available, highly selective bits and pieces, many of them taken out of context, get fitted together in an ideal or idealized, rational or rationalized, picture of what the New Man and the New Society must be. The picture may be quite attractive, even theologically sound or ideologically correct, but it is lopsided, topheavy with speculative strokes. It hardly corresponds with the experience of the Chinese people."[14]

One can hardly ignore the question which these Chinese Christians have raised concerning the gap between the image of the "new humanity" and "new society" which many Western observers of China have formed, and the reality of life in Communist China. I am certainly not qualified to judge where the truth of this question lies. However, all that seems necessary for my present purpose is the fact that most of the participants in the Båstad-Louvain colloquia have accepted the favorable reports about the "New China" as substantially reliable. My approach in this paper will be to take this view of the facts about China as a "working hypothesis." The questions I am asking could be put this way: *Supposing* that the Chinese revolution has really produced the "new humanity" and "new society" that many visitors tell us they have found there—would it be theologically sound to interpret this as an event of salvation for the Chinese people? And if so, what consequences would this have for our understanding of the Church's role in salvation history? I submit that these questions still make sense, even though, in the present state of our information, we cannot be certain that our hypothesis is actually verified.

Second Premise: A Secularized Concept of Salvation

Of the participants in the Colloquia who have seen the emergence of the New China as an event of salvation for the Chinese people, those who have most clearly explained how they understand the notion of salvation are Whitehead, Song and Madsen. While each has his own distinctive approach, and each puts the emphasis on a different facet of the complex reality, all three offer a markedly "secularized" interpretation of salvation. Whitehead suggests that his encounter with the Chinese revolution has led him to reinterpret his understanding of salvation in a secular way.[15] In Song's view, "What we have in New China is a secularized version of salvation history . . . an extreme case of the theology of secularity carried to its logical conclusion."[16] Madsen tells us: "The world itself is where the main opportunities and energies of salvation are focused."[17] For this reason, he urges us to look for "the mystery of salvation operative in the world. For secular experience is the very cradle of man as a religious being. The single most important reason for this new perspective on salvation is what might be called a rediscovery of the world."[18]

It is characteristic of those who espouse a secularized idea

of salvation to look for the mystery of salvation as it is operative in the *world* (not just in the Church); in *this* world (not just
in the next); in the *whole* world (not just in Judaeo-Christian
history, but in the history of all nations and peoples). It is also
characteristic of this view of salvation to be, as Madsen puts it,
"human-centered" rather than "religion-centered,"[19] and to
find the saving acts of God in the social and political affairs of
men, and not just in their private lives as individuals.

If we ask each of our authors more specifically how he
understands the mystery of salvation to be operative in the
world, Whitehead answers: "salvation is liberation,"[20] for
Madsen it is "humanization,"[21] while Song combines the two
ideas: for him salvation is the "freedom to be human";[22] pre-
sumably then he would agree that the process toward reaching
such salvation is liberation for humanization. As a matter of
fact, Madsen also sees "liberation" as part of the process of
humanization; thus he can speak of "the salvation through
political liberation which has been happening in China."[23] All
three of them recognize liberation from poverty, oppression and
exploitation to be events of salvation for people who had suffered so grievously under these miseries. But Song and Madsen
insist that economic and political liberation is not enough;
salvation must go on to the freeing of the human spirit, to the
breaking down of the barriers that alienate men and women from
one another and from God.

What role does God play in this process of salvation? It is
not clear to me how Whitehead would answer this question.
Song gives his answer by expressing his agreement with Schubert Ogden when he says: "What is meant when we say that
God acts in history is primarily that there are certain distinc-
tively human words and deeds in which his characteristic action
as Creator and Redeemer is appropriately represented or revealed."[24] God's action as creator is seen in those deeds by
which a people is brought out of chaos into order and stability;
his action as redeemer is seen in the liberation of people from
the bondage of such sinful social structures as feudalism and
imperialism. Madsen stresses the idea that "salvation is not a
monopoly of the Church but is given *by God* to those whom he

wills." Indeed, he insists, "The Church does not authentically attain consciousness of itself except in the perception of the total presence of Christ and his Spirit in all of humanity."[25] While rejecting an "ecclesiocentric" notion of salvation, these authors seem to me to be opting for what is really a more "theo-centric" one. God is given not a less but a more central role in salvation history, because his saving acts are seen not only in "sacred" history, but in every genuine process of liberation and humanization, even there where his very existence is denied.

What is to be said of this concept of salvation? It seems to me that it is sound, provided that one keeps clearly in mind that one is talking about salvation as a process, and not as an accomplished fact. The mistake would be to identify the state of freedom or human-ness that could ever be reached in the present world, with the ultimate salvation promised us by God; to be satisfied with anything less than that as though it were the kingdom of God already come. Similarly it would be wrong to rest content with any level of salvation that did not remain open to the transcendent value of coming to an explicit knowledge of the "one true God and him whom He has sent: Jesus Christ." But as long as one sees salvation as an ongoing process, I do not see any insurmountable objection to recognizing God's saving action in every event of human history whereby people are saved and freed from any of the various forms of bondage and oppression to which "the sin of the world" has subjected them.

*Third Premise: Recognition of Signs
of Salvation in New China*

Each of the three writers whose concepts of salvation we have discussed, finds evidence of such salvation in the emergence of the New China; at the same time, each recognizes that the salvation thus far attained falls short of being final or complete.

Whitehead, for whom salvation is liberation, asserts that "the Chinese revolution has been a genuine movement of social and spiritual liberation," while admitting that "it has been an imperfect movement, with faults and short-comings, and is far from creating a perfect society."[26] Indeed, he insists that while "salvation or liberation is not final and complete in China," it is not final or complete in any Christian community either.[27] Nevertheless, "Marxist values in China express a concern for justice, liberation and salvation to which the Christian can respond with joy and hope."[28]

In Song's view, "Salvation history in the sense of God's acts in history is intensely acted out in the transition of the old China to the New China and in the continuing effort of the Chinese Communist Party to transform man and his society."[29] God's creating and saving action is seen in bringing order out of chaos: "The order that now prevails in New China seems to reflect partially the order which God has brought into being out of chaos and disorder. The land which used to be torn and laid waste by natural disasters and by man's inhumanity and brutality has begun to function again for the welfare of the Chinese population. And society in which fear and darkness dominated seems to assume its constructive role again for its members."[30]

Yet, when Song asks the question: "Is New China the Kingdom of God realized? Does she find the way to salvation in the fullest sense of the word?", his answer is a definite "No."[31] And his reason is, that whereas "salvation is the freedom to be human," on the other hand, "when one central power dominates and dictates what a person should think, say and act, which seems to be the case in New China . . . he cannot but find himself limited in his freedom to be truly human."[32] What is now needed, therefore, is that "the acts of God in China which have taken the revolutionary movement of liberation from poverty, starvation and exploitation will now perhaps manifest themselves in the struggle for the freedom of the spirit."[33] He concludes on a note of hope for the future: "It may not be entirely wishful thinking to hope that God, the Creator and Redeemer, will chart the course of salvation history in China in such a way that the masses of Chinese people who found liberation from the evils of the old society may yet find liberation in truth and in God."[34]

Madsen finds the signs of God's gift of salvation in the "revolutionary asceticism" of the leaders of the Chinese Revolution, and in the fruits which this has borne for the people of China. By "revolutionary asceticism" he means such a total commitment to the cause of transforming social and political structures in view of an ideal society, as involves the acceptance of a life of discipline and self-denial for the sake of this cause. In Madsen's view, this asceticism has produced Chinese "who live not for themselves but for others to the point that they can face even death with a spirit of hope."[35] While admitting that not all the fruits of this have been good, he insists: "Many of the fruits of Chinese revolutionary asceticism seem to be very good: the construction of a policy in which scarce resources are distributed with perhaps an unprecedented equity, the infusion of hope and pride into a people which through most of the early twentieth century could experience little, and so forth."[36] Madsen concludes: "We do not wish to canonize China's continuing revolution. We believe, however, that the Church as the sign of the salvation of the world, should come to appreciate the good that has been produced by the 'Holy' asceticism of the men who continue to make the revolution and to learn from it and to cooperate with it and to celebrate it as a gift from the Lord of history. As for the bad—Christians should try to discern it and try to change it into good, criticizing the specks in the revolutionary history of China while remembering the beams in their own."[37]

Some Objections

The assertion that the achievements of the Maoist regime in China have involved an intervention of God for the salvation of the Chinese people, will no doubt strike many, if not most Western Christians, as the height of absurdity. It seems necessary, at this point, to consider some of the objections that these Christians would be likely to raise against this interpretation of what has happened in China.

We shall not return here to the questions that might be raised as to the reliability of our information about what is really going on in China. However, even a person who would be willing to credit the favorable reports coming out concerning the progress that has been made toward the solution of China's vast social and economic problems, might object to describing this as "salvation" for the Chinese, and even more to calling it a work of God on their behalf.

How, one might well ask, can we describe as "salvation" a revolution that has expelled the Christian missionaries, persecuted the Chinese clergy and more zealous laity, forbidden the preaching of the Gospel, made every effort to divide and destroy the Christian communities in China? If salvation comes from hearing the Good News about Jesus Christ and accepting it in faith, has not the Communist regime done all it can to deprive the Chinese people of salvation, rather than help them attain it?

The first point that comes to mind in considering this objection is that even prior to the expulsion of the missionaries, only about one percent of the population of China was Christian.

If God were even then offering to all of the other ninety-nine percent the grace by which they could be saved, even without explicit faith in Christ, then it cannot be said that by expelling the missionaries the Communist regime was effectively shutting off the only channel whereby God could offer the grace of salvation to the Chinese people.

The second point to consider is that "salvation" is a broader, more inclusive concept than just "salvation of the soul" in an exclusively religious, other-worldly sense. In the first place, it is not just the soul but the whole being who needs to be saved. In the Gospels we see that the saving ministry of Jesus embraced the whole person: not just the soul, but the body as well, when healing was needed. Again, it is not just the individual, but human society, that needs salvation. The Old Testament is the record of God's saving deeds on behalf of the whole people. The great paradigm of salvation in the Old Testament is God's intervention to save his people from bondage in Egypt and lead them to the promised land of peace and prosperity. Indeed, salvation can best be understood as liberation not only from sin but also from the consequences of sin: but sin is both private and social, and its consequences are both private and social as well.

In this broader view, we can understand that as unjust social structures that oppress the weak and exploit the poor are consequences of social sin, so the liberation of humanity from such structures, and the establishment of an equitable order of society, is truly a work of salvation for those who have been oppressed and exploited. However, one might still object to the comparison between the liberation of the Israelites from bondage in Egypt and the liberation of the Chinese from feudalism and imperialism, on the grounds that in the former case we know that God did intervene, whereas the Communist regime is avowedly atheistic, and hence one can hardly claim that God has intervened on its side.

To this one can answer that as Israel came gradually to understand that Jahweh was not just a tribal god, but the God of all nations and peoples, so also we have to understand that Christ, to whom "all power was given in heaven and on earth," is Lord not just over the "Christian" nations, but over all peoples, whether they know him as Lord or not. But this question of the reign of Christ as Lord, and the role of the Church in the spread of his reign among people, brings us to the theme which we intend to develop in the second part of this paper.

II

The Church, Sacrament of Salvation

One of the most significant contributions of the Second Vatican Council to the theology of the Church was to express the relationship between Church and salvation in terms of a sacrament and the grace of which the sacrament is both sign and instrument. In the Constitution on the Church the risen Christ is declared to have established his body, the Church, as the universal sacrament of salvation, while in the opening paragraph of the same constitution the Church is described as "sacrament of intimate union with God and of the unity of all mankind."[38]

From the latter description of the Church as sacrament, it is clear that the "salvation" which the Council had in mind has not only the "vertical" dimension of the individual's union with God, but also the "horizontal" dimension of peace and unity among all people.

One important conclusion that follows from recognizing the Church's relationship to salvation as that of sacrament to grace signified, is that one cannot simply identify "Church" and "salvation." Of course, if the Church is to be sign of salvation to the world, it must itself be a credible realization of what salvation means; it must be a visible reality of salvation in the world. But to be such a sign of salvation does not mean that it is itself the total reality of the salvation which it signifies. It is true that in the past a misguided effort to save the adage: "Outside the Church no salvation" has led to such an expansion of the limits of the Church as to equate it with the total reality of salvation in the world—as though the Church were an amorphous, all-embracing "sphere of salvation," laying claim to everything good and holy in the world as its own. Obviously, the mistake here was to identify the sacrament (which must be a visible, identifiable reality if it is to be a sign) with the thing signified, (which can well be an invisible communion of grace and charity). No, the Church, as sign and instrument of salvation, must be the visible body of those who publicly profess Jesus Christ as their Lord, who gather to celebrate this faith in Word and Sacrament, and work to propagate this faith among people. The call to membership in this community of faith is a call not only to one's own salvation, but to share the function and mission of the Church: to be, each in his or her own way, a "kind of sign and instrument" of salvation to others. But the call to salvation does not necessarily include an effective call to explicit faith in Christ and actual membership in the Church. It is true that there is a certain intrinsic ordination toward the Church in every grace that leads to salvation, but this tendency of grace, in the majority of cases, it would seem, does not reach its fulfillment in actual membership in the Church.[39]

It must be recognized, then, that salvation is a much broader, more inclusive, and less easily identifiable reality than is the Church. As we have seen also, for Vatican II it includes not only "intimate union with God" but also "the unity of all mankind." This clearly suggests a "secular" dimension of salvation, for the achievement of such unity would surely be salvation for a humanity that lives under the threat of annihilation by nuclear war.

The question that arises, then, is how the Church can be understood to be the universal sacrament of salvation, if salvation is seen to have all these dimensions: horizontal as well as vertical, social as well as personal, secular as well as religious. And even more concretely: if we admit that the emergence of the New China has been an event of salvation for the Chinese, in what sense, if any, can we claim that the Church has been the sacrament of *their* salvation?

Perhaps we could approach this question by asking how the Fathers of Vatican II understood the Church to be the "sacrament of the unity of all mankind." Elsewhere the Council says that the "catholic unity of the People of God both signifies and promotes universal peace."[40] A clue to the meaning of the Council may be found in the two verbs used here: *praesignat* and *promovet.* To justify calling the Church a "sacrament of universal peace," it suffices that the Church *signify* peace, by being a community that lives at peace within itself and with its neighbors, and that as a community it do whatever it can to *promote* the cause of peace among humanity and nations. Two limitations are immediately obvious here. The Church is not a perfect sign of peace, nor is it the only (or even the most effective) promoter of peace in the world today. The Church shares the work of promoting peace with other organizations and individuals.[41] If a lasting peace is achieved where there is now conflict or the danger of war, it is not likely that the Church will be looked on as the chief artisan of such peace. But hopefully it will have done its part in promoting peace.

These reflections on the limited role of the Church as "sacrament of peace" suggest that the description of the Church as "sacrament of salvation" should not be understood as a claim on the Church's part to be the only agent of salvation in the world. Indeed, the more broadly we interpret the concept of salvation (to include the secular as well as the religious dimensions of salvation) the greater the necessity of recognizing the limited role which the Church can play in bringing salvation to the world. For when we consider the vastness of the ills which beset humanity: the grinding misery in which so many are forced to live, the hunger even to the point of mass death by starvation, the perennial undernourishment, the illiteracy, the inhuman housing and living conditions, the unequal distribution of the world's wealth and natural resources, the oppression of weak and poor nations by the strong and wealthy, the arms race which cripples economies and threatens disaster for the whole race: —and when we reflect that humanity desperately needs salvation from all these ills—then we must realistically admit that the role of the Church as "sacrament of salvation" in all these areas can at best be an auxiliary one. The Church is called upon to *promote* salvation from all these evils, but its contribution is necessarily going to be a limited one. This should not be taken as a retreat from the strong position taken by the 1971 Synod of Bishops, who declared "participation of the Church in the transformation of this world" to be a "constitutive dimension of the Church's mission for the redemption of the human race and its liberation from every oppressive situation."[42] My intention is by no means to suggest any withdrawal of that statement, but only to stress the word "participation." The Church's mission for the redemption of the human race does indeed include its throwing its full weight into efforts for the liberation of men and women from every oppressive situation, but the Church's role as sacrament of such redemption is to be by participation. In some cases the contribution of the Church may be of considerable importance, but in others it may hardly seem to have been of any importance at all.

This brings us to the question of the part which the Church has played in the "salvation" which many Christians have seen in the emergence of the New China out of the chaos which marked the last years of the old. For it must be admitted that here, if ever, we have an instance of "salvation outside the Church," a salvation in which it would seem that the Church played no role at all. Is this an unanswerable refutation of the

Church's claim to be the "universal sacrament of salvation?"

Implications for Our Understanding of the Church as "Universal Sacrament of Salvation"

I suggest that rather than a refutation of the Church's claim to be the universal sacrament of salvation, it is a challenge to re-think what meaning this claim can have when the question at issue is the salvation of that fourth of the world's population which lives in the People's Republic of China, and when the term "salvation" is understood to have not only a religious but also a secular dimension.

In the first place, let us consider in what sense, if any, the Church can be said to be the sacrament of the "religious" salvation of the Chinese people at the present time. Here we are talking about the "salvation of non-Christians," in the sense in which Vatican II discussed this question in its Constitution on the Church. The Council teaches: "Those also can attain to everlasting salvation who through no fault of their own do not know the gospel of Christ or His Church, yet sincerely seek God and, moved by grace, strive by their deeds to do His will as it is known to them, through the dictates of conscience. Nor does divine Providence deny the help necessary for salvation to those who, without blame on their part, have not yet arrived at an explicit knowledge of God, but who strive to live a good life, thanks to His grace."[43]

Strangely enough (considering that this is the Council's Constitution on the Church), the document does not offer any answer to the question we are asking as to *how* the Church is "sacrament" of such salvation as takes place without any apparent involvement on its part. As we have seen, when the Council explained what it meant by describing the Church as a "kind of sacrament," it said that it was both sign and instrument of intimate union with God.[44] It is not so difficult to see that the Church, as the one public institution established by God as a visible sign of His plan of salvation for all mankind, can actually be a *sign* of the grace which God is offering to the

Chinese, even though the Church's presence as a sign in China itself is presently hidden. It is more difficult to see in what sense the Church is involved as an *instrument* in the salvation of the Chinese people. Or to put the question in another way; in what sense can we attribute to the Church a role of mediation of the grace which God is presently offering to the Chinese people?

Perhaps the best we can do is to say that there are good reasons to believe *that* the Church plays an instrumental or mediating role in the offer of grace to all men and women, even though it is not so clear *how* the Church is involved in this offer of grace to those people (such as the Chinese) who have no apparent contact with her. The first reason I suggest for this belief is the Pauline doctrine that the Church on earth is the body of the risen Christ. This doctrine implies an inseparable association between the Church and her Head, such that it seems inconceivable that Christ should act altogether independently of his body in exercising his saving influence on mankind. The second reason for this conclusion is drawn from the teaching of Vatican II about the analogy between the mystery of the Incarnation and the mystery of the Church. Here we see that as the humanity of Jesus is inseparably united to the Divine Word as a living instrument of salvation, so the Church is inseparably united to the Holy Spirit, serving as his instrument in the ongoing work of saving the world.[45] On this basis we can conclude that wherever the Holy Spirit is at work in the world, in some way the Church is also there as his instrument, even though the mode of this instrumentality remains obscure to us.

This should not be taken in a monopolistic sense, as though the Church were the only reality in the world which the Holy Spirit could use as his instrument in bringing salvation to humanity. The Second Vatican Council's Decree on Ecumenism states that the Holy Spirit makes use not only of the Catholic Church but also of the other Christian Churches and communities as agents of his saving work.[46] I see no reason to doubt that the Holy Spirit can and does also make use of non-Christian religions to dispose people to receive and respond to his grace. Indeed, to the extent that the "revolutionary asceticism" inculcated by the moral teachings of Mao Tse-tung has produced a generation of Chinese who really put the good of the people above their own private advantage, I would not hesitate to say that the Holy Spirit may be using the *Little Red Book* of Mao's thoughts as an instrument in leading many Chinese to a love of their neighbor, and through this to the grace of justification. (The question how love of neighbor can be reconciled with class enmity has been treated at length in some of the papers of the Colloquia).

My point here is that the claim that the Church is the "universal sacrament of salvation" does not mean that it is the only agent which the Holy Spirit can make use of in his saving work. On the other hand, it does mean that in some way (sometimes more evident, at other times hidden) the Church (being inseparably united to the Holy Spirit in a way that is analogous to the union of Jesus' humanity with the Word) is always and everywhere involved somehow in the Spirit's operation for the salvation of all people.

If one insists on having at least some suggestion as to how the Church can be a mediating factor in the offer of redemptive grace to the people of China today, one could invoke the intercessory role of the praying and suffering Church, and perhaps especially of the "diaspora" communities of Christians that survive in the Republic of China. At the level of the universal Church, this intercessory role could be seen most especially in the eucharistic sacrifice which the Church offers, every time it celebrates this memorial of our redemption, "for the salvation of the whole world."[47]

Finally, there is the question of the Church's role in the "secular" salvation which so many Christians have recognized in the emergence of the New China and in its liberation from feudalism, imperialism, and the many social ills that had oppressed and humiliated the Chinese people for the past century. Here, no doubt, the more basic question concerns the grounds for seeing this as not merely the work of human beings (as the makers of the Chinese revolution themselves believe) but also as a work of God. Or, to put the question more concretely, what connection can we show between the deliverance of the Chinese people from oppression and humiliation, and the work of the

Holy Spirit, spreading abroad the redeeming grace of Christ in the world? For if we have good reason to recognize this "salvation" of the Chinese people as a manifestation of the presence and operation of the Holy Spirit, then we can argue from the teaching of Vatican II about the inseparable union of the Church with the Holy Spirit as his instrument, that in some way the Church must also be involved in this.

It seems to me that one can argue that given the propensity of sinful human nature to egoism to the point of selfish disregard for the rights and needs of others, the emergence of a society marked by fraternity and equality, a just distribution of the necessities of life, a care for the needs of all, involves a deliverance from sinful egoism that must be interpreted as a work of redemptive grace. This grace, which the Holy Spirit offers to all, means the liberation of men and women from the power of sin (whether private or social) and from the consequences of sin (whether their own, or the sins of society, such as unjust social structures). The Holy Spirit is the agent of the liberating grace of Christ, wherever it is offered, for it is the distinctive mark of the messianic age and the reign of Christ as Lord, that now the Holy Spirit is poured out "on all flesh."[48] The expulsion of the missionaries could not accomplish the banishment of the Holy Spirit from China. We can recognize "manifestations of the Spirit" wherever we find the "fruits of the spirit"[49]—and of course the greatest of these fruits is love. To the extent that the "new humanity" and the "new society" in China is characterized by love of neighbor, we can confidently affirm that this is not a self-creation of person by person, but the fruit of humankind's cooperation with the creating and liberating Spirit of God. And if this is the case, the Church, inseparably united with the Spirit as his instrument, has also, in some way, been the sacrament of this salvation.

"Where the Spirit of God is, there also is the Church."[50]

NOTES

1. Raymond L. Whitehead, "Love and Animosity in the Ethic of Mao," *Båstad*, p. 72.

2. *Ibid.*, p. 73.

3. Jean Charbonnier and Léon Trivière, "The New China and the History of Salvation," *ibid.*, p. 108.

4. Choan-seng Song, "The New China and Salvation History," A Methodological Enquiry," *ibid.*, p. 124.

5. Richard Madsen, "The New China and the New Self-understanding of the Church," *ibid.*, p. 179.

6. Pro Mundi Vita, "China and the Churches in the Making of One World," *Louvain*, p. 28.

7. *Ibid.*, p. 29.

8. Julia Ching, "The Christian Way and the Chinese Wall," *America*, November 9, 1974, p. 276.

9. *Båstad*, p. 179.

10. *Ibid.*, p. 179.

11. *Ibid.*, p. 175.

12. "'New Man' in China: Myth or Reality?," *Louvain*, p. 45.

13. *Ibid.*, p. 47.

14. Philip Shen, "Toward a Critique of Power in the New China," *Louvain*, p. 110.

15. *Bastad*, p. 72.

16. *Ibid.*, p. 124.

17. *Ibid.*, p. 171.

18. *Ibid.*, p. 170.

19. *Ibid.*, p. 169.

20. *Ibid.*, pp. 71, 73, 78, 79.

21. *Ibid.*, p. 169.

22. *Ibid.*, p. 129.

23. *Ibid.*, p. 181.

24. *Ibid.*, p. 122.

25. *Ibid.*, p. 173.

26. *Ibid.*, p. 72.

27. *Ibid.*, p. 73.

28. *Ibid.*, p. 78.

29. *Ibid.*, p. 123.

30. *Ibid.*, pp. 126-27.

31. *Ibid.*, p. 127.

32. *Ibid.*, p. 130.

33. *Ibid.*, p. 130.

34. *Ibid.*, pp. 130-31.

35. *Ibid.*, p. 175.

36. *Ibid.*, pp. 178-79.

37. *Ibid.*, p. 179.

38. *Dogmatic Constitution on the Church*, nn. 1 and 48; W.M. Abbott (ed.) *The Documents of Vatican II* (New York, 1966), pp. 15 and 79.

39. See Vatican II, *Dogmatic Constitution on the Church*, n. 16,

which treats of the salvation of non-Christians. In the official Latin text the word used to describe their relationship to the Church is *ordinantur.*

40. *Dogmatic Constitution on the Church,* n. 13 (my translation of the Latin text, which reads: "pacem universalem praesignat et promovet").

41. The Second Vatican Council speaks of such organizations and individuals in its *Pastoral Constitution on the Church in the Modern World,* at nn. 82 and 84; Abbott, pp. 296 and 298.

42. The 1971 Synod of Bishops, "Justice in the World," Introduction; English translation in Philip Land, S.J., *An Overview,* second edition, Vatican City, 1975, pp. 74-75.

43. *Dogmatic Constitution on the Church,* n. 16; Abbott, p. 35.

44. *Dogmatic Constitution on the Church,* n. 1, Abbott, p. 15.

45. *Dogmatic Constitution on the Church,* n. 8, Abbott, p. 22

46. *Decree on Ecumenism,* n. 3, Abbott, p. 346.

47. From the prayer at the offering of the chalice in the Mass of the Roman Rite (prior to the recent liturgical changes).

48. *Acts* 2:17; cf. *Joel* 2:28.

49. *Galatians* 5:22, cf. *I Corinthians* 12:7.

50. Irenaeus, *Adversus Haereses,* 3, 24, 1: "Ubi Spiritus Dei, illic Ecclesia."

Notes on the Contributors

MICHAEL CHU, S.J. is the former Provincial of the China Province of the Society of Jesus. Currently he is director of the Society's *China Studies* and is superior of America House in New York.

JULIA CHING has taught at the Australian National University and at Columbia University in New York. At present she is associate professor of Chinese philosophy at Yale University and is affiliated with the Institute of Oriental Studies at Sophia University, Tokyo.

PAUL RULE is lecturer in history and chairman of the department of religious studies at La Trobe University, Melbourne.

ROBERT FARICY, S.J., an American, teaches theology at the Gregorian University in Rome and is the author of several books, including *Spirituality for Religious Life* (Paulist, 1976) and *Building God's World* (Dimension, 1976).

DOMENICO GRASSO, S.J., an Italian, teaches pastoral theology at the Gregorian University.

GERALD O'COLLINS, S.J., a native of Australia, teaches at the Gregorian University. He is the author of *The Case Against Dogma* and *The Calvary Christ*.

FRANCIS A. SULLIVAN, S.J., an American, teaches ecclesiology at the Gregorian University. Previously he was dean of the theology faculty there.